S0-AWC-036

To YOU We Shall RETURN

Selected Books by Joseph M. Marshall III

The Power of Four: Leadership Lessons of Crazy Horse

Keep Going: The Art of Perseverance

The Lakota Way: Stories and Lessons for Living

The Journey of Crazy Horse: A Lakota History

Walking with Grandfather: The Wisdom of Lakota Elders

To YOU We Shall RETURN

LESSONS ABOUT OUR PLANET FROM THE LAKOTA

Joseph M. Marshall III

STERLING ETHOS
An imprint of Sterling Publishing Co., Inc.

New York / London
www.sterlingpublishing.com

Library of Congress Cataloging-in-Publication Data
Marshall, Joseph, 1945-
To you we shall return : lessons about our planet from the Lakota / Joseph M. Marshall III.
p. cm.
Includes index.
ISBN 978-1-4027-3608-7
1. Dakota Indians--Social life and customs. 2. Indian philosophy—North America. 3. Nature—Effect of human beings on—North America. 4. Environmental protection—North America. 5. Environmental responsibility—North America. 6. Sustainability—North America. 7. Conduct of life. 8. Harmony (Philosophy) 9. North America—Environmental conditions. 10. Marshall, Joseph, 1945- I. Title.
E99.D1M375 2010
970.004'97—dc22

2010002992

10 9 8 7 6 5 4 3 2 1

Published by Sterling Publishing Co., Inc.
387 Park Avenue South, New York, NY 10016

Distributed in Canada by Sterling Publishing
c/o Canadian Manda Group, 165 Dufferin Street
Toronto, Ontario, Canada M6K 3H6
Distributed in the United Kingdom by GMC Distribution Services
Castle Place, 166 High Street, Lewes, East Sussex, England BN7 1XU
Distributed in Australia by Capricorn Link (Australia) Pty. Ltd.
P.O. Box 704, Windsor, NSW 2756, Australia

Manufactured in the United States of America

Sterling ISBN 978-1-4027-3608-7

For information about custom editions, special sales, premium and corporate purchases, please contact Sterling Special Sales Department at 800-805-5489 or specialsales@sterlingpublishing.com.

To my mother

Hazel Lorraine Two Hawk Marshall

Sicangu Lakota

Thank you for your love and patience

and for the examples of courage, quiet fortitude, and faith.

I hope I will one day

be worthy

of the pain

with which you brought me into this world.

CONTENTS

A PRAYER TO GRANDMOTHER EARTH

Grandmother,
You who listen and hear all,
You from whom all good things come . . .
It is your embrace we feel
When we return to you . . .

INTRODUCTION: THE HUNGER

The people could not remember how long they had lived in the wide and beautiful valley on either side of a river. But it was there that for many generations they enjoyed prosperity, for the land gave them all they needed. From the forests on either side of the river, they harvested wood to build their tools and weapons and dwellings. In the forest were herds of deer, not to mention many wild vegetables and fruits, and medicinal herbs. One day, however, came alarming news.

Hunters returned to report a strange and fearsome sight. They had seen a giant coming from the east. It was a large and loathsome creature, with two arms and two legs and a head the size of a moose, and it was very hungry. They had watched it catch and eat several deer, and it scooped fish from the streams in its enormous hands. Not only that, it had eaten entire berry shrubs—branches, leaves, and all. Though there had been stories of giants, some of the people would not believe that such a thing actually existed.

The elders sent scouts to watch the giant, and then met to discuss what to do if it was real, and if it found them and their village. They had no adequate defense against such a creature. Although someone suggested building a wall of logs around the village, it would take many, many days to do so.

A strange thing began to happen. Animals started to flee in groups and herds. Coyotes and rabbits scurried in all directions. Birds gathered in flocks and flew away. Large animals like deer and moose, and even bears, moved together in packs across the Plains, running as if their lives depended upon it. Several days later, one of the scouts returned with bad news. The giant was two or three days' travel away, and he was heading west, toward the mountains. That would bring him to the village.

But the most alarming news was the description of how the giant ate everything he could get his hands on. In disbelief, the scout recounted how the giant had left nothing but a wasteland behind him. The elders immediately told everyone to pack all the food in the village and gather their weapons. Fleeing from the terrible hungry giant seemed to be the only thing they could do.

A few men hid and waited in the hills near the village, hoping the giant would change direction and leave their homes untouched. But it was not to be. In two steps, the behemoth was across the river, and he lumbered into the deserted village. Tall as a pine, he was thick in body, and dirty, with long, tangled hair. His brow seemed frozen in a scowl above his black, angry eyes. With a vicious swipe of an arm, he caved in a house, then tossed aside logs like they were twigs as he looked for anything to eat. When he found nothing, he let out a roar that frightened all the birds in the valley into taking wing. One of the men, who had been the first to see him, indicated with some alarm that the ugly giant had grown considerably in just a few days.

In fear and disbelief, the men watched as the giant ransacked their village. By the time the sun went down, there was nothing left but piles of rubble and scattered logs. With another roar, he ran into the forest and uprooted all the berry shrubs he could find.

Thereafter the people had no choice but to flee and hide from the terrible hungry giant. There was no one who could face him, and there was no weapon that could stop him. He was much too strong. There was nothing to be done but stay hidden. In time, however, the people ate all of the food that they had brought with them, and hunting was not easy since all of the animals had fled. A wise old woman counseled that it would be safer to find a place in the wasteland that the giant had already ravaged, and hide there.

Thus it was that the people who had known prosperity in a good and beautiful land were forced to hide among the ruins of bare and lonely places where the wind moaned sadly. In time, the giant's bottomless hunger laid the land bare as far as the eye could see, and beyond.

A few of the bravest men were sent to watch the giant. They came back with a strange story. The giant had grown very large, twice the size he had been. But now he was so large that he could no longer move swiftly. Animals that he had once been able to catch with ease now outran him, and the only food he could find was plants and berries. When those were gone, he ate the grass from all the hills, and river bottoms, and prairies. His hunger was as great as ever, and though he ate everything he could get his hands on, it was not enough to sustain his great size. Before long, he grew weak, and frequently spent entire days doing nothing, simply sitting against a hill or curled up in a gully.

But his hunger did not cease, and so the ugly giant wandered looking for food, but he had eaten everything the land had to offer. He staggered about, and crawled up hills because he was too weak to walk. His stomach was so empty that to fill it he drank entire small creeks dry. The men from the village watched and soon realized that the giant's hunger had grown with his size. But there was no longer enough to satisfy him. Then, it began to rain.

Ordinarily, the rain replenished the earth, but wherever the giant had been, he had stripped it bare. When the rain came, there was little grass and few shrubs or trees to soak it up, so it flowed down every slope and gully without stopping.

Dark, gray clouds floated just above the earth, shadowy and angry, and the rain did not diminish. Strangely, there was no thunder or lightning—only steady and relentless rain. To avoid the flash floods they knew would surely occur, the people fled to high ground in the mountain foothills. Meanwhile, weak from hunger, the giant could not crawl up the slippery, muddy slopes to the top of a hill. After a struggle, he finally gave in to exhaustion and collapsed at the bottom of a gully.

Down the gully came a muddy, brown stream of water, so angry and powerful that it uprooted giant cottonwood trees.

This project is not a consequence of expertise regarding what the earth is. It was born out of a concern about the prevailing human and especially American attitude toward it. For me that attitude was summed up when I saw a bumper sticker on the back of a pickup truck which proclaimed in capital letters: WILDERNESS, LAND OF NO USE.

In other words, the natural environment does not have any value until and unless it provides for man's ease and comfort, usually by significantly and permanently altering it.

Historians hold that the so-called "clash of cultures" in North America, which began about five hundred years ago, was about possession of the land, or whose name was on the deed, as it were. Perhaps so, but it was also about attitude. Europeans and later Euro-Americans did clash with indigenous peoples over possession of the continent of North America, but the other part of that "clash" is not so tangible, not so black and white and as simple as ownership. What we tend to overlook or dismiss is what both sides *felt* about the land. On one side was a people who saw it as a commodity, and nothing more. On the other were people who regarded the land as a relative, a living entity. I firmly believe that the predominance of the former attitude is the basis for global warming and other unfortunate consequences of that mind-set, such as water pollution and air pollution.

Many of us think that the earth's natural resources are inexhaustible, or that wilderness serves no purpose in our modern world. But if we pause to consider the story of the giant, we understand that he voraciously consumed what he needed and wanted, but in the process of satisfying his hunger, he created an imbalance that eventually caused his own demise. Many of us do not think of where the materials come from when we see a skyscraper, use our laptops, or go to sleep in our beds at night, but everything came from the natural environment. Everything originates from the earth in a raw state, whether it is the sand used in concrete and glass, the petroleum used in manufacturing laptops, or the wood and plant fibers used to make beds.

There is the story of the man who was asked where milk and meat came from and who replied, "The grocery store." How many of us are like that person, seeing no connection between the products we use and consume every day and their origins as raw material? Or how many of us are like the woman who, when informed of how the staggering loss of rain forests—about a thousand acres a day—has affected the planet's production of oxygen, commented that it was none of her business because it was happening on another continent? Perhaps we have been unaware that the oxygen produced by rain forests in the Southern Hemisphere stays south of the equator.

If the harm we cause was limited to hurting humans alone, perhaps we could argue that it is justified, that we are simply reaping what we have sown. But it does not stop there.

How arrogant are we that we send a barge loaded with thousands of tons of our garbage and expect some country somewhere to take it and find a place to dump it, on their soil?

How do we explain that too many of us do not know that the meat and milk we buy in a grocery store came from animals that were slaughtered to feed us? Or that, when the amount of oxygen produced by rain forests—or any forest or tree, for that matter—decreases, we have less with which to breathe (no matter which hemisphere we live in)?

How did we come to think this way? Perhaps we do not consider for a moment that there is a finite amount of raw materials in that "useless" wilderness surrounding us. Or perhaps we are unconcerned because we have been told that all the forests will probably not be cut down in our lifetime, or all the oil consumed, or all the coal mined. But how many of us are glad that those possibilities and probabilities are for our grandchildren and great-grandchildren to worry about, that they will inherit a greater uncertainty about the point at which our inexhaustible natural resources will run out?

Arrogance and ignorance are our greatest enemies. Unless we can find a way to fight them, their adverse consequences will continue to affect the natural environment now and into the future.

The obvious cause is our consumption of raw materials. The United States is the biggest consumer in the world, using more fuel and food per person than any other country. Other industrialized nations are voracious consumers as well, but one scary projection is that global oil consumption would increase by more than 100 percent if China consumed it at the same rate as the United States. Scariest of all is that because 75 percent of the global population lives in countries where natural-resource consumption outpaces the environment's ability to renew itself, those adverse consequences will most certainly impact our grandchildren and great-grandchildren. What kind of memory of us will they have, if that is our legacy to them? Will they remember us as the generation that is part, if not at the end, of a long line of voracious consumers—merely one part of the giant who ate it all?

In terms of the cost of consumption of resources, primarily of fuel and foods but other goods as well, the United States again tops the list. Each person in the United States consumes nearly $30,000 in resources annually, followed by Luxembourg at approximately $27,000 per person per year. Switzerland and the United Kingdom are next at nearly $20,000 per person annually. On the other end of the scale (with about 120 countries in between) is India at about $2,000 per person annually, and many African countries such as Mali, Uganda, Sierra Leone, Rwanda, Malawi, and others are less than a thousand dollars per person annually.

In the category of gross household consumption, the United States is far and away the leader at a staggering $8.7 *trillion* per year. Not surprisingly other industrialized countries are also at the trillion-dollar level, though still trailing way behind the United States. Japan is at $1.9 trillion, China is at $1.7 trillion, Germany is at $1.4 trillion, India is at $1.3 trillion, the United Kingdom is at $1.2 trillion, and France is at $1 trillion annually. Below the trillion-dollar level is Italy at $920 billion, Brazil at $810 billion, and Russia at $800 billion per year.

The giant is still growing.

And it is not strictly a matter of consumption of resources. Consumption has a further impact: Think of the by-products of growth, such as the use of or production of toxic materials, as well as the effects of human habitation and infrastructures on the environment. Commerce and scenic views often seem to be the basis for deciding where to put a town or a house—but the land that is actually underneath our homes is often an afterthought.

In the early days of European and Euro-American settlements in North America, waterways were the main means of transportation for people and goods. Consequently, trading posts often sprang up along rivers, places that were initially small in size and population, and are now huge metropolises, such as Pittsburgh and St. Louis. As these settlements grew, their inhabitants used raw materials in the immediate area, such as wood, for building and fuel. Steady population growth increased the size of the village or town, which increased the consumption of raw materials.

Not only were materials depleted, but space as well. Millions of acres of former wilderness have not grown a tree or even a blade of grass for hundreds of years—smothered, as it were, beneath a building or a graveled or paved road.

Land not lost to human occupation has been polluted. For instance, it was common practice for nearly a century to dump raw sewage directly into rivers and streams. Though toxic pollution was not an issue at first, as towns became industrialized cities in the days before environmental protection laws, the amount of waste entering the rivers increased exponentially and caused irreparable damage. The water soon became caustic, foul-smelling, and undrinkable. Pollution spoiled and poisoned soil and water with all manner of waste: not only sewage, but also ordinary household products such as paint and cleaning solutions. Farm chemicals, administered to crops in order to increase their yields and satisfy the needs of a ballooning population, have also been a major source of contamination.

Perhaps the grimmest impact on our environment, and one that will be our dubious monument for thousands of years, is nuclear waste. When our flesh has long since turned to dust, the spent nuclear fuel rods and other similar products of twentieth and twenty-first century technology will still be glowing relics with a shelf-life of about twenty-five thousand years. This is our lasting legacy for future generations.

As a parent and grandparent, I do wonder what kind of world we are leaving for our descendants. Will our hunger carry over into the next generation and compel the giant to continue its wanderings over the earth, devouring every living thing it can reach? Will we condemn our children and grandchildren to consume the earth that would sustain them? Or can we teach them to banish arrogance and ignorance, learn how to honor the planet, and save it—and themselves—from destruction?

PART I

Remembrances

ONE: SMOKING EARTH

Many of us look back fondly at a particular time in our lives when we were the happiest or when life was most carefree. For me it was those years before I was sent off to school in 1953, when I lived with my maternal grandparents. I assumed that this time would go on forever because, for me, days were merely increments in the passage between seasons, and I was blithely unaware that each day represented a step away from childhood.

My playground was a 150-square-mile area of hills, gullies, meadows, and plateaus that encompassed the Little White River valley in the northern part of the Rosebud Sioux Indian Reservation. My playmates were an assortment of dogs, a few cats, and occasionally three very large draft horses. The adventures were of my own making, because I could wander and play wherever my imagination and impulse took me.

Our house stood on a rise in the middle of an open, treeless plateau thick with grass and soapweed. Below and to the west and north was the Little White River valley. The bottomland on either side of the river was the opposite of the prairie. It was a closed world choked with cottonwood, oak, and willow, and occasional thickets of chokecherry and buffalo berry bushes. It was a world of shadows, whispering breezes, silence, and solitude. On many occasions I would lose myself there. Walking quietly through the shrubbery and beneath leaves, I would often go for miles and see only a rabbit in the grass or a squirrel in the branches overhead. Hawks soared high above. If I happened to be in the right place at the right moment, I was rewarded with a glimpse of a white-tailed deer.

The river itself was, for the most part, an enigmatic old friend. My grandfather called it Makizita or Smoking Earth, its ancient Lakota name, though it was labeled the Little White on the maps. It had carved out the valley thousands of years before I was born, its waters traversing through the earth season after season, year after year, eon after eon. It told stories with its calm, soft gurgles. I yearned to understand them, sensing somehow that I was listening to a voice as old as time. Sometimes I would toss a twig or drop a leaf into its current and watch it drift away, wondering how far it would go. I surmised that it would reach the Big White River, knowing that as the chalky stream some distance to the north into which the Little White flowed. My grandfather called the Big White Maka Ska Wakpa or the White Earth River, and told me that it flowed into the Mnisose or Great Muddy, now called the Missouri River. Later I would learn that the Missouri flowed into the Mississippi River, which in turned flowed into the Gulf of Mexico. That the Little White River had those connections was mind-boggling to me later. But as a six-year-old, I was only concerned with what it was in *my* world.

In early spring and early autumn, the river's cool waters sent a mist upward. From a distance, it looked like smoke rising in the valley—thus its Lakota name. In the summers, I would wade in the cool, slightly cloudy water, and in the winter I would watch it freeze over and become a surface for the game of snow snake. After clearing away any drifted snow, I would slide long, straight willow poles toward a watermelon-sized stone placed around fifty yards away, trying to hit it. With the spring thaw, the ice would break up, cracking loudly, sounding at times almost like distant thunder. Then, the end of the thaw would fill the stream bank to bank with brown, roiling water, reminding me of the giant's frown in the stories my grandmother told. The river definitely was not friendly then, and I learned to stay away from that angry side of it.

While the groves of trees and stands of shrubs and thickets on either side were a quiet, insular world where it was easy to hide, the prairies were not. Even a six-year-old boy was often the tallest and most obvious thing around on that open, mostly flat landscape. In late summer, the wind and the extreme heat could make it downright hard to breathe. People who lived on the prairies had to learn to live with it, to accept the realities of extremes—the openness, heat, and cold. But if people were able to cope with those realities, the reward was toughness. And my grandparents were certainly physically and emotionally tough. My grandmother could walk steadily for miles and miles, and she wielded an ax better than most men. Her emotional calm came from that toughness. My grandfather, likewise, did hard, physical labor well into his sixties and seventies and exhibited the same emotional strength that my grandmother had.

In winter the prairie would assume its meanest and toughest persona. The wind would then gang up with bone-chilling, skin-biting temperatures and freeze my lungs. It was no wonder that old Lakota people told their age by how many winters—not years—they had survived. As a matter of fact, the word for year is *waniyetu*, meaning "winter." Winter had one saving grace for me, however. The deep snow enabled me to slide down the long slopes on the wooden sled my grandfather made for me. It was like flying.

In many ways winter was, and still is, my favorite season, though certainly not for the stinging cold and mean winds. During the long evenings, and often when we were forced to stay inside during a blizzard, my grandparents told stories. Not only did those stories make a howling blizzard inconsequential, they took me to moments in the past and gave me insights into the way things were for our Lakota ancestors. They brought me face-to-face with departed relatives and other people important in our tribal history, and delved into what they thought and might have felt. No other season of the year brings me closer to those memories than winter does.

Nowhere is the change of seasons more discernible than on the northern Plains, especially after a hard winter. Sometimes the change is subtle, as the snows gradually melt and days grow warmer and the land turns greener by the day. Other times, winter is reluctant to leave and heaves its last salvos of spring blizzards as a reminder of its awesome power. But sooner or later, even these last vestiges of winter gave way and spring won out, bringing its rains to renew the land. Living on a sandy plateau as we did, negotiating muddy loam or gumbo was not an issue until we had to go somewhere, and then it presented considerable difficulties. But for me it was always fascinating to watch leaves suddenly appear on the oak, cottonwood, ash, and elm trees as well as the chokecherry and buffalo berry shrubs. To a small boy, these were visible and reassuring signs. Winter was gone, and softer, warmer days lay ahead. This change was almost as dramatic as summer into autumn.

Autumn was, and is, my second favorite season of the year. The colors excited me almost as much as the first cold breezes that hinted that winter was waiting in the wings. The ultimate drama of change—of life giving way to death—was softened by the vivid splashes of color across the prairies and along the river. Orange, red, purple, maroon, and yellow leaves, along with the fading brown grasses were, and are, symbolic of life departing until the next spring. The earth was celebrating the seasons of renewal and growth that ended with autumn by painting itself in all those colors—perhaps masking its sadness. As an adult approaching autumn in the cycle of my life, I feel a strong bond with that season of the year and always will, even after winter comes. Autumn is a very profound season.

No matter the season on that plateau above the river, life for us was very elemental: There was no running water, no electricity, and the grocery store was a seven-mile trek in a wagon pulled by our big horses.

We didn't make that trip often, perhaps once a month in good weather; almost never in the winter.

Our source of water was a shallow, rock-lined well about six feet in diameter and five feet deep that my grandfather had dug. It was in the bottom of the gully west of the house where a natural spring seeped out of the ground, and its cold, clear water filled the well. Getting water from spring to autumn was not as problematic as it was in the winter. We hauled a large wooden barrel in the wagon to the hill above the well, and carried buckets up the slope. I carried a small bucket. My grandparents each carried two. Nearly twenty trips up to the wagon filled it. In the winter we had to break the ice on top of the well daily, and we hauled the barrel on a large wooden sled pulled by the horses. When one has to work hard to obtain a basic necessity every day, one dipper of water was profoundly appreciated and never wasted. The same went for food.

My grandfather plowed in the spring, guiding the single-bottom plow, which was pulled by two of our horses. With their noses low to the ground, they strained against the earth's firm resistance to the slicing blade. They turned up the soil in rows, which resembled braids. Later, my grandfather would break them down with another implement called a harrow, which consisted of long iron bars with rows of pointed teeth. After the ground was loose enough, we would mark out rows and then plant seeds. First it was potatoes, and later corn. The entire crop also included beans, peas, squash, and watermelon.

After the first sprouts broke through the earth, I began to understand—even as a six-year-old—one of the reasons my ancestors had disdained farming. A garden plot meant you were tied to one place, because it had to be cultivated, weeded, and watered. Much of that work we did early in the morning when the air was still cool.

As skillful a hunter as my grandfather was, he was just as good a farmer. He would stalk the river bottoms or wait in ambush in a blind or some gully to take a deer, especially in the fall. He attended to the garden with the same devotion to purpose. Consequently, we never went hungry.

In late summer and early autumn I would accompany my grandmother to dig *tinpsila*, a wild root vegetable. Then it was hand-picking chokecherries and plums and knocking down buffalo berries. We would lay out a sheet of canvas below the buffalo berry trees and hit the branches with long sticks, and the berries would fall. This method was out of respect for the long, sharp thorns that protected the fruit and could make hand-picking a painful process.

Just about everything that was harvested and not immediately consumed or given away—from fresh meat to vegetables to wild fruits—was preserved by air-drying. My grandmother sliced deer meat into extremely thin strips and hung them on willow frames. Corn kernels were sliced off the cob and spread out on large muslin squares. The pea-sized, almost black-purple chokecherries were pounded to pulverize the pits, and then formed into small, round patties, and then dried. Plums, which were reddish orange when ripe, were sliced open to extract the large pits then the flesh was dried. Buffalo berries were either bright yellow or orange in color when ripe and about the same size as chokecherries. Since their pits were very small, they were dried whole.

During this process, it was my job to keep the flies away and turn over the meat now and then, performing a simple but necessary task that Lakota boys had done for hundreds of generations. Knowing that did not make it any less boring, but eventually I did understand the importance of such a seemingly mundane responsibility.

Some of the freshly harvested potatoes, corn, and watermelons would be traded for sugar, coffee, salt, evaporated milk, and kerosene and other assorted supplies from one of the two stores in town. These were the supplies that we would need for the coming winter. But all in all, most of what we needed for food, warmth, and comfort through a long winter was available from the land around us, and that we acquired through our effort and hard work.

Getting through winter was the result of efforts put forth in the spring, summer, and autumn in various tasks we did. Tasks that included gathering, hauling, cutting, and splitting wood; harvesting vegetables and drying and storing them in the root cellar; rechinking the logs on the house; and others. How much food and warmth we had, and how much comfort we enjoyed, was in direct correlation to how well we completed those tasks. But it was also a direct consequence of my grandparents' knowledge of the world we lived in, and the wisdom to use that knowledge effectively. They knew its signs, tendencies, and cycles. For example, when the horses' winter hair came in earlier or thicker than usual, or when the prairie dogs fattened themselves, they knew that winter would be harsher than normal. And they were wise enough not to ignore those signs. Wisdom told them to prepare accordingly, because in their lives those tangible signs had never been wrong.

Looking back on those years in that log house on the plateau, I can say with confidence that if we had had to make do without the supplies we acquired in trade from the store, we could have. They were not an absolute necessity for survival. They were simply items that many Lakota people, my grandparents and I included, had acquired a taste for. Everything we needed—food, shelter, comfort, warmth, medicine, entertainment, and especially good health—came from the environment. It was, my grandparents reminded me frequently, the way our ancestors had lived; except for the log house, of course, and the wagon for transport. Hearing that phrase gave me a feeling of independence and empowerment, even as a six-year-old. That is probably the main reason I still cherish those years of my childhood and still think they are my favorite memories.

My grandparents and the land, the environment around us, taught me that there are several kinds of power. In particular, I learned to respect the power of the changing seasons. For me as a child, two seasons held the power of nature within them: summer brought thunderstorms and tornados, and with winter came blizzards. Those were the very symbols of life and death. A thunderstorm, a tornado, or a blizzard can take your life, or, at the very least, wreak havoc upon it. But they can also teach you to fight for life, to grasp its fragility and appreciate that it is precious.

TWO: THE MAN WHO PLANTS SEEDS

During those years with my grandparents, everything I did, felt, saw, and tasted was assessed by my limited experience and imprinted on the blank canvas of my mind. Yet, I also saw the land and its plant and animal inhabitants through the eyes of my grandparents. They expressed opinions and reactions to the things they saw, and they told me about their experiences from before I was born. Furthermore, their vision of the land and their perception of it was not limited to their own lives and experiences. They were, in turn, influenced by their parents' and grandparents' cultural and experiential perspectives.

Looking back now, it is obvious that my perception in the1950s and that of my ancestors in the 1850s of the *same* land was different in many respects because of how we lived on and interacted with it. There was basic and accurate knowledge of the 1850s and on because the stories from my grandparents and other Lakota elders were very vivid. They described such activities as hunting, moving camp, cutting lodgepole pine in the Black Hills, tanning buffalo hides for tipi covers, harvesting wild fruits and vegetables, making tools and utensils from wood, bone, and stone. They also told stories specifically of the northern part of the reservation immediately after it became a reservation, and before. They, like practically everyone in their generation, knew which individual or family used to live where and for how long, and who was buried where. They knew where the government pastured the issue cattle, which were eventually butchered and distributed to families in a particular district. "The man-who-plants used to live there," one of my grandparents would point out, for example. Of course they used the Lakota word *wojuwicasa* (woh-joo-we-cha-shah). It meant literally a "man who plants seeds." Another connotation, used for the Bureau of Indian Affairs (BIA) subagent who lived among the Lakota people out in the districts, was "boss farmer," because it was his job to teach hunters how to become farmers.

In the 1950s, on all the Sioux reservations in South Dakota, we Dakota, Lakota, and Nakota people did categorically the same things as our nomadic ancestors did to survive—we worked to make a living and built shelters. But the extent and kind of activities were significantly altered by the consequences of the so-called Indian wars of the northern Plains and by U.S. government policies and control, which began in the late 1870s.

By the mid-1870s, the vast herds of buffalo on the Plains were virtually extinct and no longer a dependable resource. That altered more than diet. In late 1877, the Lakota people were relocated from two agencies in northwestern Nebraska Territory to the Great Sioux Reservation in Dakota Territory—the western half of the present state of South Dakota. Most of them gravitated to their ancestral territories. Thus four large separate reservations were created west of the Missouri River: Standing Rock in the north, partially in what is now North Dakota; Cheyenne River adjacent to and below it; Pine Ridge in the southwest; and Rosebud east and adjacent to that. Decimation of the buffalo eliminated hunting as the primary activity by which Lakota males provided for their families, forcing them to become farmers. At the same time, the annuity beef cattle provided by the government were never available in sufficient numbers to adequately replace the buffalo as a food source. The quality of the meat was also generally poor, stringy, and insubstantial.

Though Lakota men hunted, mostly deer and small game, to augment food supplies, it was not the same as it had been when game was plentiful and hunters could range far and wide. Although many Lakota men preferred firearms because of expediency, bows and arrows were still crafted and used after the establishment of reservations. But hand crafting those weapons soon became a lost art, just as buffalo hunting occurred only in memory.

My grandfather hunted primarily with a small-caliber rifle and managed to kill enough deer to significantly augment our winter food supplies. He knew how to make bows and arrows and was quite skilled as an archer. Furthermore, he had comprehensive knowledge of the practical and cultural significance of the bow and arrow. He was one of a few. But overall, in the 1950s, the bow and arrow were little more than novelties for most people. Things had changed—the Lakota lifestyle had changed—and consequently there had been losses. The bow and arrow were in that category, as was the buffalo hide lodge, the tipi.

Near extinction of buffalo meant more than the loss of a primary food supply. It also meant the loss of materials for tools, toys, household items, and lodges. Twenty to twenty-five tanned hides were required for the outside covering of one lodge, and ten for the inner winter or dew lining. By 1880, lodge coverings made fifteen to twenty years earlier—when fresh hides were still available—were showing signs of wear, and new coverings were made of canvas. When the various Lakota bands scattered to different parts of the Great Sioux Reservation, log houses began to appear. But it was a common sight to see buffalo or canvas lodges pitched next to them, a juxtaposition of tradition and grudging change.

Movement in pre-reservation times occurred because of practicality, which led to a lifestyle. The bison moved in vast herds across a vast landscape, so our Lakota ancestors became nomadic hunters, even before the arrival of the horse. But practicality was dictated by the flow of seasons and availability of resources. Because harsh weather and deep snow made moving camps difficult in the winter, people simply broke up into smaller groups and found likely places near water and game trails to locate a village, and stayed there through the winter. After the arrival of horses the need for young cottonwood trees was an additional consideration, because horses could augment winter feed by eating cottonwood tree bark. When the weather improved in the spring, the various scattered winter villages reunited into one large community that stayed together until the next winter.

But even during good weather, villages moved frequently to procure food and to accommodate the social and political interactions with other villages. After our ancestors acquired horses, finding good grazing was a constant necessity. So when an area was grazed down, the village moved to another place where good grass was available. Sometimes, however, the urge to move became too strong to ignore. Consequently it was not unusual for a family to take down its lodge, pack it and their belongings, and strike out across the prairies to visit relatives somewhere. Neither was it unusual for an entire village to suddenly decide to move for no other reason than to savor the journey, to see what lay over the horizon, to enjoy the ultimate freedom of the nomadic lifestyle.

Reservations with boundaries limited that freedom somewhat, although within those limits people still wandered, especially in that period from the late 1870s to about 1910. I remember the stories of people on the Rosebud Reservation moving up and down the Little White River valley, from where it entered the reservation from Nebraska to where it emptied into the Big White River, a distance of roughly a hundred miles. Belongings and family were piled into wagons, although those who did not have a wagon used the drag poles, or travois, pulled by a horse. Migrating up and down the valley was the last vestige of freedom, a taste of the old days when the freedom to move defined a culture.

Unknown to most of the Lakota in 1887, the U.S. Congress had taken steps to eliminate that freedom with the Dawes Severalty Act (or General Allotment

Act), named for its main sponsor, Senator Henry Dawes of Oklahoma. That act changed collective ownership of reservation land to individual ownership. A census of the Lakota was taken at the same time the reservations were surveyed and divided into 160-acre parcels. When the census was completed, all males eighteen years of age and over were allotted land. Married men were given 160 acres (a quarter section), and single men 80 acres. For the most part, women were not given land.

The allotment process was finally completed around 1910 and "surplus lands" were opened for homesteading to Euro-Americans. Theodore Roosevelt, a supporter of the Dawes Act, stated that it was a "vast pulverizing engine to break up the tribal mass." Many native people of the time, the Lakota included, did not understand what the Dawes Act was. They did know that white people had done something to change their lives again, after thirty years of reservation life. Virtually overnight, white people moved in and the reservation maps began to resemble checkerboards with Indian lands adjacent to homesteaded lands. Perhaps that was what Roosevelt meant. On the Rosebud Reservation, families could no longer pack up their belongings and wander up and down the Little White River valley, because they might trespass on someone else's property. Emotions usually ran high when such trespass was across white homesteaded land. Thus the last taste of freedom derived from wandering over the vast prairies was gone.

The great nomads of the Plains were no more. They were relegated to 160-acre plots of land, and their only consistent travel was a few miles to the issue station. There the once-daring hunters who had chased buffalo on horseback at thirty miles an hour across the prairies collected their rations of beans, flour, salt, and stringy beef. The only viable connection to the past was the land itself.

Oblivious to the legal constraints on the land imposed by the U.S. government through the BIA, the environment cycled on. Seasons came and went, rivers flowed, and the wind blew. The tangible symbols of the new order were probably more painful for the Lakota, who took umbrage on behalf of Grandmother Earth. Fences and roads were the most obvious. Next came the agency towns, the headquarters of the BIA on each reservation, where its central administrative authority was located and staffed by whites. All of these were constant reminders that someone else was in control, making the rules for how the Lakota should live their lives. But even those tangible, insidious symbols could not alter the spiritual connection the Lakota had with the land. Try though they might (and did), that connection was one aspect of the old life that the BIA—and white society as a whole—could not destroy.

From the allotment period on, Lakota people acquiesced to the reality that land had to be treated as deeded property. They regarded that as a superficial imposition by the whites, who did not understand how things were, how things had been long before they appeared. Though they followed the rules, nothing could alter or interfere with the respect the Lakota people felt for Grandmother Earth. It was the classic "smile and nod" approach because there was no other choice.

Therefore, while I was having boyhood adventures, playing along the river and roaming over the hills and prairies and all the while having my own reactions and forming my own perceptions of the physical environment, my grandparents were—in a manner of speaking—whispering in my ear. They told me of the places they had lived as children with their parents, and as a young married couple. They told me about various landmarks that were significant to their families, to the community, and to the Sicangu band. Just as important, they told me where their parents and grandparents had lived, where they had died and were buried, and of the stories and information they had heard from them. And through those whisperings, the ancient connections to the physical environment were passed on and reestablished for one more generation.

My grandparents' descriptions of the land were always very vivid, sometimes more so than descriptions of people or animals—so much so that rivers, creeks, gullies, hills, and prairies had moods, personalities, and tendencies. To them, and hence to me, the land was alive. I was connected to it. It was connected to me. But not all Lakota young people were influenced as I had been. Due to the persistent efforts of the U.S. government, Lakota culture became less important to some Lakota people. Consequently, the sense of connection to the land became weaker and weaker with each passing generation, and the new perspective—that land is property—became more and more acceptable.

Thankfully, the ancient cultural relationship to and with the land has not been totally eradicated, but the new perspective has taken enough of a hold in Lakota hearts and minds that now there is more than one way to look at the land. For some there is a deed with descriptions of property boundaries. For others of us there is still Grandmother Earth.

THREE: ICEWINSKAS!

Because of the traditional Lakota values that shaped my grandparents, they doted on me and tried—within reason—to fulfill my boyhood whims, which was what all Lakota grandparents and parents did. In fact, the Lakota village characteristically raised every child in it. That had changed somewhat in the 1940s and 1950s, however. The community, by and large, no longer lived in a village. In that part of the reservation, families were scattered up and down the Little White River valley, each living on different plots of land allotted to male heads of households in 1910 by the BIA. (This was the case on all reservations in South Dakota.) But there was still a community, a village in concept and function. The only thing separating us was distance.

For example, my grandfather's two sisters (my grandmothers) and their families lived north of us. One of my grandmother's half brothers lived two miles west of us along the river bottom, and several of her cousins lived nearly twenty miles south. Of course there were also those who were distantly related to us, or friends who were not related to us at all. So, all in all, the village comprised several hundred people scattered far and wide, but it was still a village.

Religious gatherings, social occasions, funerals, and weddings were the usual reasons people would get together. Those times were opportunities to see and visit with people we had not seen in weeks or even months, sometimes a year or two. But outside of these kinds of occasions, families and friends also visited each other regularly. One grandfather, a widower, would trek across miles of prairies and hills to spend a day or two with us, always bringing food. Furthermore, it was not unusual for relatives to suddenly appear, often coming with the entire household traveling in a horse-drawn wagon. My grandparents were always happy to have visitors. Food, good conversation, and storytelling were always the hallmarks on such visits.

Topics of conversation were everything that was life: family, the weather, births, deaths, marriages, crops, hunting, white people and their things and ways, the Indian Bureau, cattle and horses, and the land. Now and then, there was talk about how things had come to be the way they were in the 1950s.

By then the reservations in South Dakota had been in place for nearly eighty years. In late 1877, people of the seven Lakota bands were relocated from the agencies near Fort Robinson, Nebraska, to the Great Sioux Reservation in Dakota Territory. The various bands gravitated to different parts of the region. My maternal ancestors—the Sicangu Lakota or Rosebud Sioux—occupied a central triangular area bordered on the east by the Missouri River and down to what would be the Nebraska border—ancestral territory, as a matter of fact. My grandparents' generation, those people in the fifty- to seventy-year-old age range, were the children of those who had been the first generation to give up the nomadic hunting life to become sedentary farmers.

Large-scale farming was obviously not part of the pre-reservation lifestyle. My ancestors had developed ways to thrive within the parameters of the physical environment, and did so for many generations after migrating onto the Plains. Hunting was the way to procure most of the food and much of the materials for shelter and clothing. Planting was usually limited to plots of corn on river bottoms in the spring, and left to the unpredictable moods of the weather and wild animals. If anything grew, it was harvested in the fall.

Farming on a larger scale was a necessity for survival within the forced parameters of reservation life. Planting crops became the primary source of food, and it became necessary to do so year after year and on a scale that would ensure high yields. Though farming was unusual and even strange to them at first, they did it because they had to, and in doing so they exhibited a characteristic that life in general as well as the environment itself had taught them: adaptability.

Several stories suggest that the Lakota—before they were known as such—had migrated south to the lake region of what is now Minnesota. Prolonged and unusually harsh winters in their former homelands caused a severe shortage of food, and forced the people to seek a more hospitable environment where game was available. In the heavily forested region of thousands of lakes, they adopted a primarily sedentary lifestyle. Hunting, however, was still the preferred method of procuring much of their food. Fishing became a close second, and they also harvested the abundance of wild fruits and vegetables, including wild rice. Overall, life was good, until European involvement in tribal differences—rather than weather or a catastrophic event——caused them to relocate again.

Of the indigenous groups in the lake region, the Dakota and their Lakota and Nakota relatives were the newcomers, and prior inhabitants were not thrilled with their arrival and encroachment. In time, hostilities developed with the Ojibwa (also known as the Anishinabe or Chippewa). Those people developed a trade relationship with another group of newcomers, the French, who had guns to trade. Using the advantage of their new weapons, the Ojibwa forced the Dakota, Lakota, and Nakota out of the region. So they went west.

The Dakota and Nakota chose the grassy, rolling hills east of the Great Muddy, or Missouri River, in what is now eastern South Dakota. The Lakota continued farther west across the river and moved onto the open prairies, eventually establishing a territory reaching west to the Big Horn Mountains, north to the Yellowstone River (in Montana), and south to the North Platte River (in southern Wyoming).

For the Lakota, the open, rolling, and virtually treeless prairies west of the Missouri River were much to their liking. They adapted to that environment by returning to their ancient lifestyle of nomadic hunting. But that change was not arbitrary. It was dictated by the wide open, beckoning land and the bountiful herds of bison, more commonly known as buffalo.

The bison were large ungulates, with the adults weighing from a thousand pounds to a ton and standing nearly six feet at the shoulder hump. They became the ultimate resource for the Lakota, a source of meat as well as clothing, robes (coats), lodge coverings, tools, toys, weapons, glue, rope, utensils, and so on. And they were nomadic, moving in vast herds, so the Lakota became nomadic to make use of this seemingly endless resource.

Hunting bison, at first without the use of horses, was not an easy task. Hunters dug pits or built blinds (huts of concealment) using grass and shrubs in and along bison migration routes, and shot them with arrows or impaled them with lances at extremely close range. Some daring men donned wolf hide capes and crawled close to and often among the grazing bison, knowing that cows would not readily retreat from lone wolves, thus providing the opportunity for close-range shots. A favorite wintertime method was for hunters on snowshoes to drive bison into deep snow, where they floundered and could be dispatched at close range. These methods were not abandoned when the horse appeared, contrary to some assumptions. The horse did enable the harvesting of dozens if not hundreds of animals in a few days, and certainly made the hunt more exciting.

These stories containing historical and cultural information were told in bits and pieces over the course of years. As a younger child I was entertained by them. In my early teens, however, I began to wonder why we no longer lived in tipis and hunted buffalo. How, I wondered, did all that come to an end?

It was not an easy story for my grandparents to tell. But tell it they did, once again in bits and pieces, but this time I suspect it was to lessen the frustration, disappointment, and pain, and perhaps the confusion.

The gist of the story was that strangers came, a different kind of people—with attitude, as it were. What's more, there were more of them than there were Lakota, more than all the ordinary human beings on the Plains combined, as a matter of fact. To make matters worse, they had an endless supply of weapons that were superior; from six-shooters to cannons (called wagon guns by the Lakota). Furthermore, they had the railroad, which enabled them to haul people and goods rapidly over great distances. The telegraph enabled them to communicate rapidly over great distances. This technology, unknown to the Lakota, gave the strangers an insurmountable advantage.

Those strangers came to take and occupy the land, killing Lakota people to do it. Those who survived would change, from what they wore to what they believed and how they looked at the land itself and related to it. Land became property to be divided up, fenced, and farmed. No wonder, I realized as a young adult, that the stories of the old, nomadic hunting life were told with such reverence and nostalgia. I began to understand the sadness I saw in the eyes of many of the storytellers.

Some would say, "Icewinskas!" (ee-che-ween-skash) after finishing a story. This is a phrase that is hard to translate literally, but it is akin to "Incredible!" It is used when something is difficult, if not impossible, to believe. Some of the old storytellers had a hard time believing their own story of change. "Icewinskas," they would say, and sadly shake their heads.

At some point I realized that the period before the coming of the strangers was, to my grandparents and great-grandparents, comparable to my carefree childhood. It was, for them, the best of times. That is not to say there were not problems and hard times, but whatever life put in their path they were able to confront it without interference, because they were meeting the challenges of life on the open plains as a free people. My parents and I, on the other hand, were born into a Lakota world under the control of the strangers whose avowed policy and mission it was to remake us into their image. Our world was one of square houses, English language, Christianity, a diet heavy in fat and refined sugar, wool and cotton clothing instead of tanned hides, religious and government boarding schools, and wheeled transportation. My generation was taught to be careful and wary of white people, even deferential, because it was they who were in control.

My grandfather plowed the land and planted crops, and he harvested in the fall. He built a log house and fixed the barbed wire fence that bordered and separated our quarter section of land from the next.

He greased the axle hubs of our wagon and oiled the leather harness the horses wore to pull it. Yet he did not do these things because he accepted the values of the culture that forced the Lakota to change; he did those things because they were necessary for his family to survive. Many Lakota fathers and grandfathers did the same.

"Hecetuwelo (heh-che-doo-weh-loh)," he would say, meaning, "That's the way things are." The reality of survival for him was different than it had been for his father. He learned to farm though his father never had to. If there was any sense of resistance to plowing and planting, I never heard him give voice to it. He accepted the way things were. But there was one thing that did not change for either of my grandparents: their reverence for the land.

My grandmother's land was marked on a flat map by dotted lines, and in the physical world its border was a wire fence. It was regarded as property by the culture that had imposed the lines and the fences. To my grandparents and to me, however, it was home. Just as important, it was part of their identity, not because they owned it but because it was a living, viable entity. Rarely did she refer to it as "My land." She always referred to it as *Untipi kin el*, or "Where we live." In her view and my grandfather's view, it was we who belonged to the land.

Unfortunately, belonging to the land is no longer a predominant reality among the Lakota. Legal and practical issues have diluted the spiritual connection to Grandmother Earth, such as tribal sovereignty, civil and criminal jurisdiction, and just maintaining a land base. It is a double-edged sword. Those issues arise from the fact that there still is Indian-owned and -controlled land. All native or indigenous tribes must remain ever vigilant and thwart every attempt to erode tribal sovereignty and our land base. Significant loss of either will mean no land to belong to.

Belonging to the land is not an operative concept in Western cultures. The opposite is true: The land is to be owned, used, and controlled to the primary benefit of the owner. Along with ethnocentrism, owning, controlling, and profiting from the land has been the reason for conflicts between human beings since prehistoric times.

Lakota author Luther Standing Bear expressed his culture's relationship to the land succinctly in 1933 when he wrote:

> *The Lakota was a true naturist—a lover of Nature. He loved the earth and all things of the earth, the attachment growing with age. The old people came literally to love the soil and they sat or reclined on the ground with a feeling of being close to a mothering power. It was good for the skin to touch the*

> *earth, and the old people liked to remove their moccasins and walk with bare feet on the sacred earth. Their tipis were built upon the earth and their altars were made of earth. The birds that flew in the air came to rest upon the earth and it was the final abiding place of all things that lived and grew. The soil was soothing, strengthening, cleansing and healing. [*Land of the Spotted Eagle, *1933]*

This was not to say that the Lakota saw the necessity of controlling a certain territory in order to use the resources therein—such as water, plants, and game—to make a living. Furthermore, the ancient Lakota did take action to affect the land, such as establishing trails, burning off old grass to help replenish growth of new grass, or cutting down young pine for lodgepoles. But such actions did not necessarily mean that they saw themselves as having any kind of power greater than the land. They saw the land in the same category as air and water, neither of which could be owned. Thus, laying claim to a certain territory was not the same as ownership. They did not see the land as property or commodity, but as a living resource with cycles of renewal—a resource to be used, but also to be truly appreciated and respected. To take Luther Standing Bear's sentiment a step further, the land—Grandmother Earth—was the very symbol and example of generosity, illustrated in the simple but wise comment of a grandmother to a grandson.

Generations ago, before the coming of horses, a group of Lakota people were moving camp somewhere on the prairies west of the Great Muddy (Missouri) River. As they came to a smaller river to cross it, they saw that a large herd of bison were already there and crossing. The herd was so large that the people had to wait most of the day for it to pass. A young boy expressed his frustration and impatience, wondering if they would ever see the end of the seemingly numberless herd.

"Be patient," advised his grandmother. "The last animal will eventually cross the water. While you are watching them, remember that you are seeing how the earth can be endlessly generous. Be sure your generosity is the same."

Such stories told in the 1940s and 1950s were an indication that the ancient association with the land was not entirely forgotten, that the land was so much more than property to be owned or a commodity to be used up, in spite of the new order imposed by the BIA. It was, to my grandparents' and parents' generations, still a living entity that was an integral part of their cultural identity and the values they held dear. As Luther Standing Bear said, "The old ones came to literally love the soil and they sat or reclined on the ground with a feeling of being close to a mothering power." It was that "mothering power" that undoubtedly helped teach the ancient Lakota that family and community were critical to their survival and strength—just as much as food, shelter, and clothing.

Therefore, as a child, I reaped the benefits of that strong sense of family and community in the way my grandparents enabled my childhood to be carefree and taught me what I needed to know, and in the way other relatives and elders—the village or community—contributed to my upbringing in spite of being spread out over miles and miles.

To my grandparents and to the community, the village, in those years of my childhood, and the connection to the land was still strong. Unfortunately, it was also that period when those strong ties were under intense assault.

FOUR: LOOK BACK AND REMEMBER

The assault to eliminate the ancient Lakota connection to the land was essentially a three-pronged effort of *attitude*, *policy*, and *action*. The effort was effective.

The BIA and certainly white America at large looked on Indians as a lesser, primitive, people defeated by a superior and more enlightened race and therefore subject to the whims of the victor. Even when the Cherokee Nation in the east won their case against forced removal from ancestral homelands in the Supreme Court in 1828, President Andrew Jackson disdained it. Referring to Chief Justice John Marshall, he arrogantly remarked, "Let him enforce it." Jackson's attitude represented that of the majority of white Americans. Consequently, everything about Indians—cultural values, tribal lands, traditions, spiritual beliefs, customs, and language—was regarded as archaic and uncivilized and subject to change. First and foremost was land and religion. (As so aptly stated by Vine Deloria Jr., "At first they had the Book and we had the land. Now we have the Book and they have the land.")

Attitude drives everything else, including policy and action. The U.S. Congress was well aware of the prevailing attitudes of white America, especially the sense of "Manifest Destiny," the apparent God-given right of Euro-Americans to conquer and assume control over the continent (to the point that there were discussions over the conquest of Canada and Mexico). Since Manifest Destiny became a reality and Indian tribes and nations were defeated and subjugated in the process, their territorial and spiritual ties to the land were of little or no consequence to Congress. Though several treaties identified and established territories for certain tribes, i.e., the Fort Laramie Treaties of 1851 and 1868 for the Lakota et al., they were later significantly altered or abrogated in favor of the United States when critical resources were discovered on the land, such as gold or silver. It was the policy of Congress to protect the rights of the United States. In 1875, a year after an Army expedition into the Black Hills affirmed the rumors of gold, a so-called agreement was enacted that removed the entire western third of the Great Sioux Reservation, identified in the Fort Laramie Treaty of

1868. That third contained the aforementioned Black Hills.

If policy separated Indians from their lands, it was also the thrust of separating Indians from their cultures, which included changing their values regarding land. Indians of many tribes agreed, for the most part, with the Judeo-Christian teaching that God created the earth. But the idea that man should have dominion over the earth was antithetical to the ancient reality of human interaction with the land. Divergent as Indian lifestyles were across the continent—some were hunters and gatherers, some planted and raised crops and hunted—they, for the most part, did not see themselves as apart from or above the natural environment. The power they saw in themselves was not in their ability to dominate the land, but to coexist with it because they knew and understood the environment so intimately. But after generations of white mainstream influence, and as Christianity gained more and more of a foothold, the ancient beliefs of man's interaction and relationship with the earth began to fade. The concept of man holding dominion over the earth was accepted alongside other Christian beliefs.

Fortunately, the conversion of Indians to Christianity did not totally eradicate Indian culture, for two critical reasons. First, not all Indians accepted Christianity and chose instead to keep their traditional beliefs. Second, some Indians converted to Christianity to more or less "go with the flow." They went through the motions, but inside they clung to the old ways. Consequently, traditional beliefs were quietly passed on, and customs were practiced secretly.

Nevertheless, the laws and regulations governing the reservations could not be ignored, especially with regard to land. They were in force and enforced no matter what Indians thought or felt. On reservations across the United States, several hundred tribes were faced with the daunting and often traumatic process of learning to survive and function in a new culture. So, for the most part, the past and ancient lifestyles took a backseat to issues of the moment, such as finding employment, a different system of educating children, forming tribal governments, or facing racial prejudice. Individuals, families, and communities had to adjust and acculturate almost on a daily basis. There was little choice but to acquiesce to the process, but in spite of that many stubborn traditionalists taught their children and grandchildren—often and necessarily secretly—how it was in the old days. Thus the ancient beliefs of coexistence with the land were not entirely lost.

On the other hand, because of the persistent influence of the mainstream culture, for some Indians those ancient beliefs were relegated to the shadowy margin of awareness, where they remained for several generations. For some they remain there still, and for others they are entirely forgotten. Many times old ways give way to new ways. Everything moves on with the inexorable march of progress.

Aspects of progress do serve the greater good—the discovery of a vaccine to eradicate a deadly disease, or smoke alarms, for example. But in our rush to embrace the new there is always the inherent danger of discarding something valuable simply because it is old (throwing the baby out with the bath water, as it were). Perhaps most of us are quick to embrace the next newest idea, or product, or technology simply because we have forgotten where we have come from.

For us indigenous people of North America, where we have come from is both geographical and experiential. Many theories have been advanced and debated about the place from which we may have originated. Some think our ancestors crossed a land bridge from Asia. But what is infinitely more important than our geographical origin or even the date on which we may have arrived is what we did—how we survived and thrived—after we came.

During those years with my grandparents on our plateau above the Little White River, my grandfather frequently took me for walks. He enjoyed those walks, as I did, and at first I never considered that there was a purpose aside from sheer enjoyment. We walked during any time of the year, through the summer grasses or on the winter snow. Many times we would take a break from a chore, such as gathering firewood, and strike out across the prairie or over a hill.

Just about every time he would have us pause at some point. Then he would take me by the shoulders and gently turn me around. "Look back at the way we came," he would say. "Remember it." I would nod dutifully, not really knowing why he told me to look at our back trail.

Sometime during the year I was approaching my seventh birthday, we went on one of those walks. It was in the autumn and the trees and grasses were wearing their bright colors. He stopped beneath a towering cottonwood tree and asked me to turn around, and look back at the trail we had walked. As I had done several times before, I complied with his instructions. But I had been thinking about those instances, and I finally screwed up my courage to ask why.

"Why are you telling me to do that?" I asked.

His reply came quietly, but it has never faded in its significance.

"Someday I will send you back down some trail by yourself, and if you do not remember the way you came, you will be lost."

⌗

The trail that our indigenous ancestors have walked for thousands of years before the arrival of Europeans is not inconsequential history. It may be a key to the future of this continent, if not the entire world. By the time Europeans arrived, indigenous people were already established in every part of two large continents: North and South America. There were hundreds, if not thousands, of different tribes, and most of them were thriving.

Like humans living anywhere on the planet, the pre-European people who populated North (and South) America experienced floods, drought, famine, and conflict. Survival was not easy by any means. Yet every part of the North American continent was inhabited, from the frozen Arctic to the north to the jungles of what is now Central America in the south. Some societies flourished more than others, but all found ways to make the best possible use of the resources available to them.

Scholars who study the pre-European history of North America have more or less decided that the continent is separated into twelve culture areas, separating one from the other on the basis of terrain, resources, flora and fauna, and climate.

Perhaps just as significant as the fact that our indigenous ancestors populated every part of this continent is the diversity of lifestyles that developed. Generally speaking, societies were either nomadic or sedentary and made a living by hunting, gathering, or farming. But our ancestors did not choose their lifestyle—unless they migrated to an entirely different region. In a very real sense, the lifestyle was dictated by their environment. It is the classic example of blending, of adapting, of coexistence.

No matter who we are and what our ancestral origins might be, most of us are not curious about the lifestyles and the lives of our ancient ancestors. Very likely there are those of us who pity them because they—in our perception—did not have it as good or as easy as we do, considering all of the technology and modern conveniences we now enjoy. Perhaps in some sense we might even regard our ancestors as inferior. We should not, however, forget that they did indeed function and survive with less than we have. And, in the same situation, we would have done the same.

How we evolved as indigenous inhabitants of North America is more than a story of confrontation or conquest, or the imposition of political ideologies or religious beliefs. It is a record of how many different cultures of people of the same race developed separately from one another while using the same basic approach in their interactions with the natural environment: We based our beliefs on the realities we saw in that environment, and lived by them.

FIVE: THE SLIVER OF THE NEW MOON

This statement is often made in an offhand manner: "The continent of North America was already inhabited when Europeans arrived." Even when Euro-Americans began to genuinely acknowledge this fact, history books rarely addressed the fact that those inhabitants had an established relationship with their environment, or that they were thriving in a world that had no need of newcomers. Instead, the usual characterizations remain: *primitive*, *Stone Age*, or *savage*, among others. But the fact of the matter is that the native people who, in a state of shock, watched those newcomers raze a patch of forest to accommodate their needs and their lifestyle had long before found the key to survival in that same environment. They had adapted to it and were appalled that human beings could so drastically and rapidly change it to suit themselves.

Centuries were to pass before Europeans and Euro-Americans would begin to objectively study the lifestyles of the people who had preceded them to North America. That objectivity would finally, to some extent, transcend the two extreme characterizations that had been formulated about indigenous peoples here: On one hand the natives were thought to have lived a utopian lifestyle in total harmony with Mother Nature—the *noble savage* concept. On the other hand, they were not much better than wild animals, human beings in form only and without souls. Neither stereotype allowed for indigenous people to have the capacity for emotion and reason. For example, initial reaction to the discovery of mounds such as the Great Serpent Mound in Ohio and the Great Mother Mound in Mississippi was that they were intrusive; that is, the prevailing opinion was that they were built by non-indigenous people, and possibly—probably, according to some—by Europeans. But when such stereotypes and ethnocentric reactions were debunked and disproved, scholars began to realize that the indigenous people of North America had millennia of experience and knowledge from living in and with the natural environment.

Archeologists have found evidence that North America's indigenous peoples survived and thrived in every part of the continent. As anthropologists got into the act, scholars began to look at the obvious factors of terrain, climate, weather patterns, and physical resources, and saw the continent from their perspective: not as sharply delineated countries, states, and provinces, but as several distinct *culture areas*. The distinctions were drawn because of different indigenous lifestyles. For example, people who lived in the desert Southwest built dwellings of stone or mud and wood and wore clothing woven from plant fibers. The people in the Arctic constructed dwellings out of snow and ice in the winter, reindeer hides in the warmer months, and clothing of various kinds of animal hides.

If pre-European North Americans did arrive from elsewhere millennia ago, they obviously encountered flora and fauna that were both familiar and unfamiliar. As difficult as it undoubtedly was to acclimate and adapt to a new environment, it was not impossible for these people, because they possessed skills and abilities that enabled them to survive on an elemental level. Furthermore, they possessed the trait to blend in with and accept the realities of the physical environment. In their time (as it is now), humans were not the fastest or strongest of the creatures that inhabited the land. Therefore, it was far more sensible to blend in with and adapt rather than attempt to change or overpower anything, including the environment. Sometimes a fast-flowing river or a glacier simply could not be crossed, or a woolly mammoth was too belligerent, and living to hunt another day was far more sensible.

It was this intangible sense of reality that pre-European North Americans possessed, and it was every bit as instrumental to their survival and evolution as any technology they possessed. As a matter of fact, new developments in technology were few and far between. For example, a wooden lance sharpened to a point was the standard for tens of thousands of years, until a stone point was attached. Therefore, proven approaches and methods were probably equally as important as any new weapon or tool. The development of stone tools, implements, and weapons was probably regarded as something that increased the odds of survival, and it probably did not foster an immediate sense of power over other creatures or the environment. Obviously, without weapons or tools of any kind, chances of survival were radically reduced. Because of that reality, a new or improved weapon or tool was likely regarded for what it was: a better chance of survival, and nothing more.

My grandfather taught me this basic attitude about relating to the physical environment I grew up with. As a boy on the Rosebud Sioux Indian Reservation in the 1950s, I learned it by crafting a wooden bow.

His choice of wood for a bow was a young ash tree. It was the best available in our part of the northern

Plains, I learned later. Young oak, before the stalk thickened, was also good, as was a straight chokecherry stalk. If at least one bow was to be made from it, the wood had to be at least as tall as the person who would use it, and the same thickness as a grown man's wrist. A young tree the size of a man's forearm could make as many as four bows if it was split correctly, and skillfully, once it was dry.

Preferably, the bow tree was cut in the winter because the sap was down, which we did in this case. Because my grandfather wanted to speed up the process, he chose a very slender tree so that he could work on it immediately. According to him, a green tree was softer and easier to carve, as opposed to a stave that had dried for three to four years. After we cut the chosen tree, he peeled off the bark and went to work immediately.

In a matter of hours he shaped the green wood into a bow, using a large, two-handled woodworker's drawknife he had made and a wood rasp (an iron file used on wood). When he was satisfied with the shape, he then built a fire outside and hung the bow on a platform high above the flames. There, after several more hours, the bow slowly dried. After that, he attached a sinew string and tested the flex of the limbs and shaved them with the edge of a piece of broken glass until they bent uniformly. He was finally satisfied and declared the bow finished when it resembled the sliver of a new moon.

Of course the process tested the limits of my six-year-old patience. I was eager to shoot it, and when I was eventually allowed to do so, it performed flawlessly. At that age I knew the basics of using the weapon: placing (nocking) the arrow on the string, pointing the bow hand (holding the bow at the handle or middle) toward the intended target, drawing (pulling back) the string, aiming, and releasing. I imagined myself stalking a white-tailed deer in one of the draws by the river, and killing it with one arrow. I felt powerful and could hardly wait to go hunting. But in reality, each arrow I released rarely hit the same spot twice. Soon enough, I was frustrated and even thought something was wrong with the bow. At that point, my grandfather stepped in.

He patiently told me that the bow did not make me a hunter, or even a good marksman, simply because it was in my hands. Other things were necessary, according to him, and hunting on my own was not in my immediate future.

For the rest of the winter, whenever the chores were done and nothing else needed our attention, we prowled the gullies and groves of trees for miles on either side of the Little White River. I was shown the trails used by deer: hoofprints in the snow and dirt and matted earth or snow where one or two had bedded down for the day. My grandfather also showed me what shrubs and plants deer ate in winter and how their grazing patterns differed the rest of the year. He also pointed out likely spots to build a blind, as well as how to blend into the landscape or the shrubbery to ambush any approaching deer. But, unfortunately, the snow melted and spring came before I could do any hunting. During the following spring and summer I spent every available moment practicing with my bow, so by the time autumn came again, I was a bit stronger and somewhat more proficient with my bow.

For the ancient hunter, knowledge was just as important as skill with a weapon. I sometimes got the notion that my grandfather considered knowledge more important. Skill with the bow and arrow enabled a man or boy to make superb shots, but it was useless, according to my grandfather, unless he knew where an animal would be. That was why my grandfather had been careful to teach me about the seasonal habits and habitat of the deer. He also told me to study the land in every season of the year. The river valley, for instance, did not look the same in winter as it did in summer. There were other changes as well. If the winter was hard and deep, it would become difficult for deer to scrape away snow in order to find grass, so they would feed on the bark of cottonwood saplings instead. Therefore, in a hard winter, it served the hunter to remember where the saplings were along the creek and river bottoms.

My grandfather's attitude and philosophy toward knowledge of the land, the trees, plants, and animals was not something he had acquired alone. He learned it from his father and stepfather primarily, and from all of the other adult Lakota males who had influenced him. And, in turn, they had learned it from their fathers and grandfathers, and so on. The other males in our extended family on the Rosebud Reservation had the same attitude, which was logical. My grandfather's generation of Lakota men were the sons and grandsons of those who had been nomadic hunters. Hunting was how they provided food and shelter for their families, and how well or how poorly they did so was in direct relation to their knowledge of the same things my grandfather tried to teach me.

Years later, after I had learned that there were more native peoples than we Lakota and our friends and enemies, and that these native peoples lived in all parts of the North American continent beyond the Great Plains, I wondered how they had lived before white men came. I wondered if all Indians chased buffalo on horseback and lived in hide lodges. But when I began to learn about other native nations and tribes, I was astonished at the diversity. Though those people had to concern themselves with the same basic issues of food, shelter, and clothing in order to live, they went about it in so many different ways. I learned that there were some in the north who hunted caribou and lived in houses made of snow and ice. In the forests to the east, some hunted elk and lived in longhouses made of wood. In the western mountains, some pursued mountain goats and sheep and had dwellings similar to my Lakota ancestors. I was astonished to learn that Indians who lived along the northwestern coasts made long wooden canoes out of giant pine trees and used them to pursue whales on the ocean.

I knew that the lifestyle of my ancestors as nomadic hunters evolved because of necessity and adaptation to the physical realities of the natural environment. When the Lakota came to the northern Plains and found it full of buffalo, a meat pack that migrated great distances, they had to go where the food went. It was a logical reaction for me to assume, and hope, that those caribou and whale hunters and those people in the east who planted great plots of corn lived the way they did for the same reason—that they, like my ancestors, lived with the land and not apart from it. The more I learned, the more I realized that the lessons of my grandfather—to know the land—had been taught by other grandfathers among all of the other native peoples who populated the land that some called Turtle Island. I felt reassured and connected because the more I learned, the more I felt a kinship with others who knew and understood the realities of the physical environment—the land and its inhabitants—and found ways to live within those realities.

Embracing the way things were regarding the land was adaptation, not dominance. That was the common philosophy that connected the diverse indigenous cultures and peoples who populated the entire North American continent for thousands of years before Europeans came. They stood in humility before the awesome power of Grandmother Earth.

I realized that we—my generation of Lakota, as well as other native tribes and nations—were the beneficiaries of the values that had existed and evolved for countless generations: a set of values learned, affirmed, and applied by each succeeding generation. My grandfather's simple lessons in knowing the land were a time-tested reality for all native peoples.

The off-handed statement that North America was already inhabited when Europeans arrived, therefore, has a backstory. In fact, the people who were already in North America possessed real knowledge about their environment. Further, the philosophy that enabled them to coexist with and adapt to that environment predated European settlement or the Eurocentric attitude that the indigenous North Americans were primitive, uncivilized, and unintelligent. The newcomers' main goal was to own and control the land and the resources on it, and that meant pushing aside the previous inhabitants. In the process they also pushed aside invaluable knowledge that would have benefited them and the land they so coveted. In the process, they also failed to learn the critical element: respect. Rarely have human beings, individually or collectively, respected anything that they own or can control. Property can be prized or cherished, but that does not necessarily mean it is respected.

Having a healthy respect for the natural environment in which they survived and thrived did not mean that indigenous people were "tree huggers," or that they lived in a utopian setting of abundant flowers, rainbows, and waterfalls. For example, though they knew the necessity and benefits of rain, they probably did not like a violent downpour or even a dismal, steady drizzle. And no one, now or then, enjoys the onslaught of mosquitoes or any kind of biting insects.

Respect comes from intimate knowledge and deep understanding, and it is the basis for the customs, practices, traditions, and values that comprise culture. It enables societies to function and evolve, and it certainly is the basis for the spiritual connection that indigenous peoples felt to their world. When a people respect their environment and feel genuinely connected to it, it is easier to adapt and coexist. In many instances they emulated characteristics of animals, not so much to mimic them, but to use those characteristics in ways that enabled their own survival.

Northern Plains hunters, for example, knew that one or two wolves were not a significant threat to herds of bison. When a wolf or two approached a herd, the bison would simply form a circle and keep an eye on the intruders. The hunters too would crawl toward the bison herd, imitating the movements of a wolf while camouflaged beneath a wolf hide, holding a bow in one hand and arrows in the other. Within twenty to forty yards a bison could be successfully brought down. This is but one example of many illustrating how respect leads to adaptation.

But there was a more effective and important consequence of respect: It prevented arrogance. Humans could not prevent floods, blizzards, tornados, mud slides, prairie fires, avalanches, and droughts. But they could survive or avoid them if they knew the circumstances under which they might occur. In other words, they did not try to circumvent the power of nature, they simply and logically adapted to it.

Much has been lost as a consequence of five hundred years of interaction between the indigenous inhabitants, Europeans, and Euro-Americans. Language, traditions and customs, beliefs and values, not to mention most of a continent, have been lost. However, the most profound loss is rarely, if ever, considered important enough to warrant more than a passing mention: As indigenous cultures became diluted and diminished and nearly destroyed, so too was respect for the natural environment. Fortunately, that cultural aspect has not entirely been lost.

Perhaps that grain of awareness is enough to start again. *What one man can do, another man can do*. After all, tens of thousands of generations of indigenous people in North America survived and thrived with that knowledge. The value of that knowledge is still relevant today. Intimate knowledge of the natural environment—its whims, cycles, patterns, seasons, terrain, and topography—became second nature to them. Such knowledge can again be the key to our survival as humans, but this time, instead of adapting to the environment in order to maintain our existence, we must save and heal the wounded earth so that future generations are assured of survival.

To accomplish this, we must go back to the beginning.

SIX: FENCES

We are often taught that fear is a negative emotion. It is often associated with greed, anger, and cowardice. However, part of our nature as humans is to fear anything that is bigger or faster or more powerful. It is a survival mechanism, and if it had not served us well, we would be extinct due to our own ignorance and stupidity. Fear is also a natural precursor to respect—only when we have honestly and realistically assessed the source of our fear can we can acknowledge, more fully understand, and even honor it.

Respect often occurs when we learn, sometimes the hard way, that we cannot control or overpower everything. When that happens, we are more cautious in how we interact with what we cannot control or overpower. Only those who are foolish or arrogant ignore that reality.

But foolishness and arrogance are also part of our nature, and too often they circumvent respect. Furthermore, those behaviors are often based on illusion, not reality.

In this day and age, we are frequently told that the natural environment is powerful, harsh, and unkind. We see and hear examples of that power in news broadcasts or see documentaries about devastating tornados, hurricanes, avalanches, floods, earthquakes, brush fires, mud slides, and droughts. Some of us have experienced the most debilitating effects of the power of nature firsthand as victims of natural disasters. But, for many of us, direct contact with nature is infrequent, and inconsistent. We live and work and play inside structures that shut nature out, and we travel in vehicles that do the same. The trails and paths we walk are marked and paved.

We cannot imagine our towns and cities without paved streets, and the great interstate highway system was already in place when the current generation of Americans was born. We do not know of a time when "I-5 or I-90 or I-35" was not part of everyday conversation. Or when city traffic interchanges such as Dallas's High Five were not part of the city skyline.

Seventy-five percent of Americans live in or near cities and are in constant direct contact with an environment that is a product of technology—an environment that suggests power over and control of the natural environment, reinforced by skyscrapers, bridges, subways, and airports. Even when we leave the boundaries of the city, we are faced with superhighways, jumbo jets—about four thousand in the air at any given moment—and hydroelectric dams. We have developed a sense of pride in this society and our ability to fashion a world conducive to the comfort and convenience of modern humans. And, perhaps more than we realize, we have acquired a sense of arrogance and power in spite of the fact that most of us are only the beneficiaries of technology. We may take advantage of it, but most of us did not build it.

As a case in point, a modern hunter uses a high-powered rifle on which is mounted a state-of-the-art telescopic sight. This weapon system enables him to kill game animals at distances of up to several hundred yards. His contribution to the process is the ability to buy the rifle and scope and a certain amount of skill and effort to use it. Though he had nothing to do with the idea, design, and manufacture of his weapon system, he nonetheless feels powerful because of it, and perhaps somewhat arrogant at his killing shot at five hundred or six hundred yards.

Of course, many of us are not big-game hunters, but we are nonetheless enamored with the power of technology to the point that it overwhelms the necessity of learning about the natural environment. The first inhabitants of North America, on the other hand, knew full well that nature was much more powerful than they were. Obviously, the technology available to them was not nearly on the scale that we have today, and it did not develop at light speed as it does today, and therefore did not cause burning ethical issues such as cloning and stem cell research. But it is their sense of realistic awareness that we need to emulate, and it very well may help us with the ethical issues we face.

Perhaps to acquire, or reacquire, our sense of realistic awareness, we need to know and understand the kind of world in which our indigenous ancestors lived. What was the natural environment of North America, or, as some indigenous people called it, Turtle Island?

Pristine is the first adjective that comes to mind. The landscape was uncorrupted and unsullied. Of course we must understand that it was man who would do both the corrupting and sullying. So, in this case, *pristine* is synonymous with an environment unaltered by humans. But that still does not completely answer the question.

I recall vividly my grandfather's frequent wistful stares across the prairies. I wondered what he was looking at, or for, or what he was seeing that I could not. One day he answered my unspoken question by stating out loud that he wished that fences had never been invented. It was the one symbol of the non-Lakota (and non-Indian) lifestyle that he disliked the most. I share that sentiment to this day, and my feelings are fueled by hours and hours of imagining what the plains looked like without fences, without cornfields, vehicle trails and roads, and high line and telephone wires. As a boy growing up on the Rosebud Reservation and playing on, in, and around the varying topographical features along the Little White River, I most enjoyed those moments when I found myself someplace where there was no sign of human habitation or passage: those moments when there was no road in the distance, no fences, no houses, no domestic cattle or any sign of ranches or farmsteads. Over time, I visited those places again and again because the perspective they provided seemed, to me, to be of the real world—an unspoiled and untainted world, as it had been for thousands and thousands of years.

North America is the third largest of the seven continents, and contains every kind of terrain, land formation, and geographical feature found on the planet: mountains, plains, coniferous and deciduous forests, swamps, deserts, rivers, canyons, glaciers, waterfalls, jungles, lakes, inland seas, fjords, bays, short and tall grass prairies, volcanoes, and rain forests. It stretches from the top of the world nearly down to the equator.

For indigenous people who lived on and moved across this vast land, respect for it had to have come easily. One only has to stand at the rim of the Grand Canyon, hear the thunderous roar of Niagara Falls, watch clouds floating around the twenty-thousand-foot summit of Mt. Denali, or search for the end of a vast arctic ice field that stretches beyond the curve of the earth to understand how the ancestors must have felt. No wonder they thought of it as a living and viable entity. And beyond the awe-inspiring physical characteristics were the factors that could cause harm and hardship—and did for any who were not knowledgeable or experienced, or who were unlucky—such as blizzards, floods, extremes of cold and heat, tornados, hurricanes, and numerous other powerful and unyielding occurrences.

But we modern humans who seem easily awed and give our respect to the Hoover Dam, the Golden Gate Bridge, the Empire State Building, and other products of human effort and technology, can still understand, even to some small degree, why the indigenous people of North America felt the same about their natural environment. The only difference is that they probably did not suffer from arrogance because they knew they had nothing to do with the creation of a gorge, or a waterfall, a burning desert, or giant redwood trees.

The most important consequence of respect for an

unyielding and powerful environment was the ability to live and function and be humble within its parameters. It was the single most important key to survival. It was more sensible, for example, to find a suitable place to cross a stream than to put people at risk in a strong current. It was more sensible to respect the power of the stream, for every individual in the family and community unit was critical to survival, and the loss of one person affected everyone.

There was plenty of risk from predators, extreme weather conditions, and hunting, as well as myriad other hazards. Therefore, it was preferable to minimize risk by approaching every situation with common sense and humility. But it is basic human nature to take risks, to push to the edge of safety and reason. There were those, of course, who took risks for the sake of taking risks, but more often than not, they paid the price with disappointment, embarrassment, injury, or death.

Respect for the environment probably prevented the ancestors from thinking that they could change the environment to suit their needs. It was much easier to adapt themselves to it. Therein lies the basis for indigenous perspective in North America.

My Lakota ancestors were living on the northern Plains at the time of first contact with Europeans. The Plains were but one of the *culture areas* that directly influenced the lifestyles of indigenous inhabitants.

It is, I believe, necessary to know something of each culture in order to understand how and why cultures are different. Just as importantly, we must understand how and why indigenous people formed an enduring spiritual bond with Grandmother Earth.

Most scholars agree there are at least twelve culture areas across North America where the study of pre-European indigenous people is concerned. They include:

Arctic

Touching three oceans—the Pacific, the Arctic, and the Atlantic—the Arctic culture area reaches from extreme eastern Siberia (part of the present-day Russian Federation), across northern Alaska and Canada to the western coast of Greenland.

Subarctic

This culture area stretches across the entire North American continent, from the Pacific to the Atlantic, covering much of Alaska's interior and most of Canada.

Northwest Coast

Bordered on the west by the Pacific Ocean, this area reaches from southern Alaska to northern California, a distance of two thousand miles.

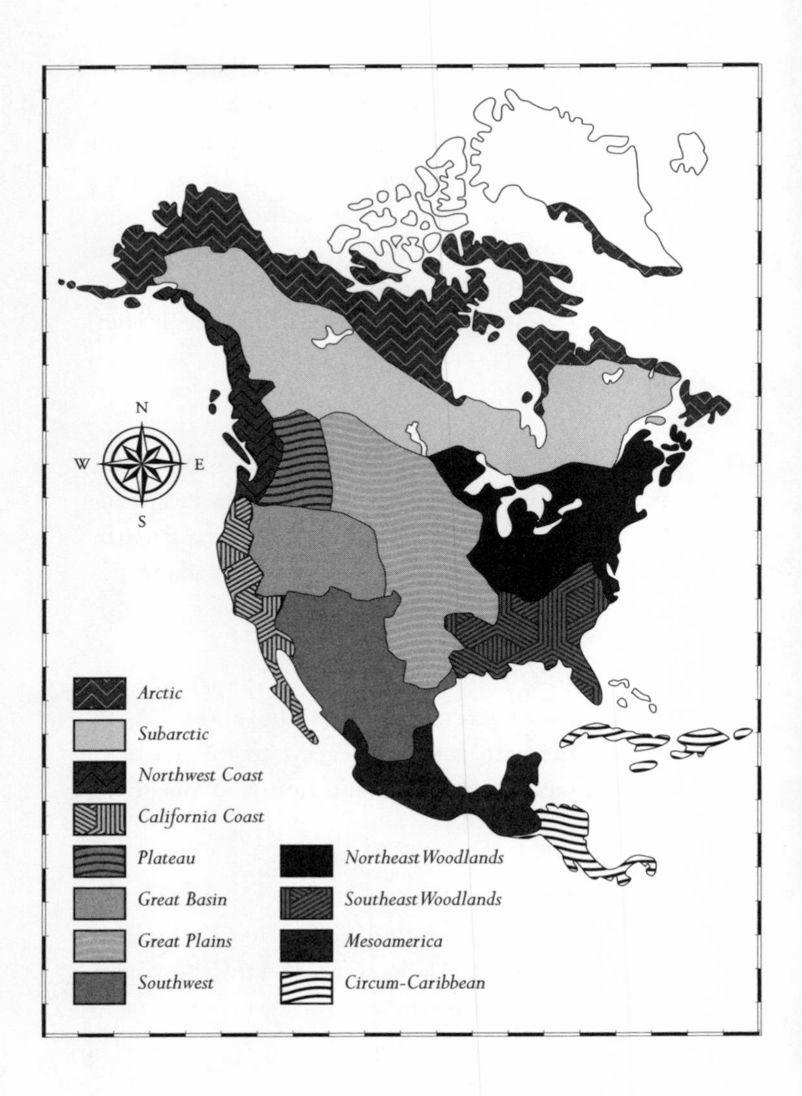
N
S
E
W
Arctic
Subarctic
Northwest Coast
California Coast
Plateau
Great Basin
Great Plains
Southwest
Northeast Woodlands
Southeast Woodlands
Mesoamerica
Circum-Caribbean

California Coast

From northern California to the tip of the Baja Peninsula.

Plateau

Numerous waterways and drainages are the greatest feature of this area, which encompasses what is now eastern Washington, central and northeastern Oregon, southeastern British Columbia, northern Idaho, and western Montana.

Great Basin

Just below the Plateau an enormous desert basin encompasses southeastern Oregon, southern Idaho, western Wyoming, western Colorado, all of Utah and Nevada, and a sliver of northeastern California.

Great Plains

From southern Texas north to southern Manitoba, southern Saskatchewan, and southern Alberta, and east from the Mississippi River Valley westward to the Rocky Mountains, the Great Plains are second in sheer size only to the Subarctic.

Southwest

From central Mexico, the Southwest culture area stretches north into a portion of west Texas, most of

New Mexico and Arizona, and the southeastern tip of California.

Northeast Woodlands

From the Atlantic Seaboard west across a portion of Canada to northeast Minnesota, south along the Mississippi River Valley to eastern Missouri and then east across the Appalachians and Tennessee to the tidewater region of North Carolina. This area includes ten major rivers and the Great Lakes.

Southeast Woodlands

Bordered on the north by the Northeast Woodlands, this culture area stretches south to encompass all of Florida and west to east Texas, touching a portion of the Great Plains culture area.

Mesoamerica

From the southern tip of the Southwest culture area, Mesoamerica encompasses the rest of Mexico and includes all of Guatemala, Belize, El Salvador, and parts of Honduras, Nicaragua, and Costa Rica. It is bordered on the west by the Pacific Ocean and on the east by the Gulf of Mexico.

Circum-Caribbean

The eastern portions of Nicaragua and Costa Rica and

all of Panama are part of this culture area, as are all of the islands of the West Indies; from the Bahamas and Cuba to Grenada and Trinidad and Tobago.

⌗

No matter which part of the continent we live in, it is difficult for most of us to visualize a map of North America without the current national, state, and provincial boundaries, or the jagged lines of roads and highways and the dots and squares that represent towns and cities. As children of our modern era, we cannot think of the natural environment without some indication of human passage, imprint, or habitation. How many of us look at the condensation trail of a high-flying airliner and regard it as an intrusion?

Likewise, there are many paintings of rural scenes depicting various kinds of terrain or topography, and they are called *landscapes*. Yet in such paintings there are almost always indications of man, be it a rotting fencepost, a rusting truck body, a well-worn trail, or a small cabin by a lake—objects so familiar to modern viewers that they seem almost as natural and picturesque as wind-worn logs or the new growth of vegetation in the spring.

Necessarily, we show maps of the past with shaded indications of current boundaries so that we can have a reference. Most, if not all, of us have no concept of how the land was before man put his stamp on it. In the 1994 feature film *Geronimo: An American Legend*, a white character shouts at Geronimo: "There was nothing here before us; there'd be nothing if we left it to you." He was, of course, talking about the land, and the mind-set that the land is nothing unless man—in this case, white men—do something with it. WILDERNESS, LAND OF NO USE, remember.

How many of us, I wonder, truly give any thought to the reality that the natural environment existed long before humans became humans? Nature existed without our presence and our help. Therefore, the land predates us by several billion years and North America existed for those billions of years without a name, without maps, and of course, without us. Can it last billions more with us?

SEVEN: BUFFALO WOMAN

Memories of childhood with my maternal grandparents on the Rosebud Reservation are a welcome and easily reached retreat from the demands and routines of the present. We all have memories of what gave us our start in the world, how we began as individuals. If we choose to do so, we can remember the people, the circumstances, and the places that shaped us and gave us our identity. In a larger sense, we can look back and understand how we found our identities as members of a community or society.

While people, places, and specific events helped make us the people we are today, as individuals, we probably consider one factor most important among the others. For me the most influential factor has been people—those who were part of my extended family. The most influential were my maternal grandparents. A very, very close second behind people is *place*.

The place that immediately comes to my mind is that plateau above Makizita Wakpa, the Smoking

Earth River, now known as the Little White River. That plateau has no name that I am aware of, but it was my home, the one that I remember most fondly. Although I do have memories of other places earlier in my childhood, that plateau where I lived with my grandparents was part of the most formative years of my life. It is where they built a house and planted a garden, and where we lived as a family. My childhood emanated from there—it was the center of my physical existence. I felt safe and secure as I stood on that plateau and began to wonder what lay over the horizons around me. It was the place I first wandered away from home alone, knowing it would be there to welcome me back when my adventure was done. It welcomes me back even now when I think of my boyhood years, and I feel empowered by those memories.

Home is or should be that way for all of us. Consequently, if one person feels that way, it should be natural for a community or a society or any group of people to have a strong, emotional connection to a home place, a homeland. For my mother's people, the Sicangu Lakota, it was the area west of and adjacent to the Missouri River, in a rough triangle bordered on the south by the Niobrara River, or Running Water River, in Nebraska, north to a point near the town of Fort Pierre, South Dakota. Of course, when they claimed and occupied that area, the names were

Mnisose (for the Missouri River), Mni Kaluza (for the Niobrara River), and Wakpa Sica (meaning "bad river") for the Bad River near Fort Pierre. Our relatives the Hunkpapa (Sitting Bull's people) and Mniconju Lakota were to the north. Intermingled with them were the Itazipacola, Oohenunpa, and Sihasapa Lakota bands. The Oglala were as far west as what is now north-central Wyoming.

As a culture, we Lakota are identified with the northern Plains, that open land of flat prairies, occasional buttes, and numerous creeks and rivers, burning hot in the summer and dangerously cold in the winter. Any land shapes character, and ours was shaped by those extremes. Unbending and unyielding land forces the beings that live in it, above it, and on its surface to be strong, or die. And often we have a tendency to identify most with the thing that is hardest on us, that pushes us to our limits. It was certainly true in our case. The same is true for all the indigenous people of North America, whether they lived in the forests, on the tundra or the mesas, or along the wild and windy coastlines. There is no place like home, and that connection is obviously reflected in a Lakota creation story.

The short version is this:

Long ago, it was said, the people resided inside the earth. They would look out from the hole in the earth and see what life was like on the surface, and they wanted to live under the blue sky and fair winds and among the trees and the grasses. So they climbed out, emerging to a new life in the open, except for one person, a woman. She stayed behind, remaining beneath the earth.

Life turned out to be good for the people on the surface. There were many fruit trees and plants for them to gather, and plenty of animals like the deer and elk for them to hunt. So the people prospered and became many, and grew into a strong nation. However, years of plenty came to an end when drought visited the land. In the springs and summers there was no rain, and very little snow in the winter—not enough to replenish all the things that grew each spring. Soon there was little for the animals to eat, so they moved away. All of this, of course, meant that the people had practically nothing to eat.

The people suffered, became ill, and many died of starvation. The woman who stayed behind looked out and saw what was happening, and her heart broke. She prayed to the Great Spirit for help, and was guided out to the surface. There she turned into a great animal, the pte, *also called* tatanka*—the buffalo. Soon enough, the buffalo became many and were so plentiful that the people hunted them and lived. They prospered once again, much more than they had before, and became an even more powerful nation. So grateful were they to the great animal* *that saved them that they called themselves* Pte Taoyate, *the People of the Buffalo, or the Buffalo Nation.*

The hole in the earth in which the people in the story lived is said to be in the Black Hills, specifically the cave that is now the main attraction at Wind Cave National Park. No one knows for certain when the Lakota first inhabited the Black Hills region, but it is a well-known fact that the buffalo, or American bison (*Bison bison*), was the primary reason the Lakota culture flourished on the northern Plains.

In cultures the world over, adversity is an important element in many stories. Famine, drought, flood, and pestilence in one form or another are severe hardships that people must endure. Adversity is an important element because people or societies that endure it emerge stronger and wiser. Adversity leads to rebirth. Where indigenous peoples of North America are concerned, times of trouble also lead to the reaffirmation of the connection they have to the natural environment.

For several Plains tribes, the affirmation of that connection is observed in a ceremony that is still performed today. The Lakota call it *inikagapi* (ee-nee-ga-gah-pee), which means a sweat bath (a wet sauna). Some Lakota think of the word as "to make life again." The word *ini* comes from *wiconi* (wee-cho-nee), or "life." Hence the ceremony now known as the sweat lodge is conducted as a renewal, a cleansing, or rebirth. Other tribes have their names for it, of course, but for the Lakota, the ceremony correlates to the story of the people being reborn to a new and different life when they emerged from the earth. This leads to the other critical aspect of connection to the earth—the sense of identity.

For all intents and purposes, the earth gives birth to the people in the story. They are born into a new life when they emerge from the underground to the surface. However, they do not disconnect completely with the "womb," the earth, because they remember where they came from: one of them remains behind. Consequently, there is still a strong connection, and that is symbolized in the structure now known as the sweat lodge, as opposed to the ceremony itself.

The lodge is a circular dome, a low framework of poles covered by hides. It represents the female womb—in this case the womb is the earth itself. As an object, it is a tangible reminder of the connection that exists between the natural environment and the various forms of life that exist, including us humans. The ceremony of Inikagapi takes us to the next level of that connection: the spiritual bond, a connection much like the umbilical cord that connects mother to child. Though it is cut after birth, the essence of that connection always remains. There is nothing more powerful than the bond between mother and child. Hence, for us Lakota traditionalists—and all native traditionalists who practice their specific tribal spiritual beliefs—that bond with the earth is very real.

For me, as a participant, the ceremony of Inikagapi is one of rebirth. I enter the lodge burdened with cares and woes and emerge renewed—reborn, in a sense. But more than that, I feel a powerful sense of connection. That feeling is not limited to the people with whom I shared the experience of the ceremony, but extends to everything that is, and to the one reality that connects us all: the earth. Every thing, every being that exists and has ever existed, is born of the earth.

But the Inikagapi also reminds me of home, the place that had a significant role in my formative years, and is undeniably part of my identity. Even the slightest thought of home invokes images and memories of my grandparents, parents, and relatives, not to mention numerous experiences. Inseparable from all of that are the sights, sounds, smells, tastes, and textures of that plateau, the river and its valley, the hills, meadows, gullies, and creeks. Vivid is the sound of the wind over the grass and through the branches of cedar trees, the painful stab of prickly pear cactus, the sweet scent of peppermint, a slightly tart newly ripe plum, the cool shade beneath a tall cottonwood tree, and the soothing caress of the river's current over my bare feet.

The sense of place for native people is both broad and specific. From the single and unique perspective of each of our particular tribes or nations, we identify with this continent of North America. Though we speak many different languages and observe and practice different traditions and customs, we all think of the land as mother or grandmother. In the north, the Inuit and the Iñupiat identify with the tundra and its expanses of snow, or a whale surfacing for air at the edge of an ice floe. In the Southwest, the Hopi and Diné (Navajo) and Zuñi revel in the scent of piñon or in the panoramic vision of purple or blue mesas shaded in the distance. For the Huron or the Potawatomi or the Susquehannock there was probably nothing to compare to the protective embrace of the endless forests. Furthermore, indigenous people were not just moved by beautiful scenery or emotional attachment to a particular feature or location—they felt a reverence.

That reverence for place is manifested in the number of areas and landmarks considered sacred by North American indigenous people. There is no way to have an accurate count of the sites considered sacred, but suffice it to say there are thousands. Some are historically well known, such as the mountain in Alaska called Denali (Mount McKinley), or Taos Blue Lake in New Mexico, or the Black Hills in South Dakota. Other sites that may be familiar to non-native people are

Mount Shasta, California; Bear's Lodge (Devils Tower), Wyoming; and the Pipe Stone National Monument, Minnesota. To be sure, there are many sacred sites not known to non-natives, and they probably never will be. Be that as it may, no matter where such places are, they epitomize the spiritual relationship indigenous people had with the land. Those waterfalls, caves, buttes, mountain peaks, mesas, rivers, lakes, and so on, will always have a special place in the hearts and minds and spirits of the people who revere them as long as tribal identities are tied to the land.

Place and *identity* are synonymous for indigenous people, and non-native people can nominally connect the names of indigenous cultures to parts of the North American continent. For example, the word Eskimo conjures images of the frozen Arctic, polar bears, harpoon-wielding natives paddling after whales, dog sleds, and dwellings made of ice and snow. Likewise, the name Algonquin invokes pictures of forest-dwelling people with houses made of wood or bark, long bows, and birch bark canoes, while the Hopi, Anasazi, and Zuñi are immediately associated with the desert, Monument Valley, and cliff dwellings. The names Makah, Coastal Salish, and Chinook bring to mind oceangoing wood canoes, totem poles, and large plank houses overlooking the rugged Northwest coast, and so on. For the indigenous people, however, the relationship to the land is much more than geographic. We take pride in being known as "desert people" or "people of the longhouse" or "snow walkers" or "people of spirit lake," or whatever other labels non-natives know us by. But the core of that identity comes from generations of being shaped by that environment—be it the tundra, the desert, the plains, the mountains, the forests, the rivers, or the ocean. We are of the land as much as any other creature or being is—whether it is the bison, the wolf, the deer, the rabbit, or even the mouse. The land—the earth as a whole—gave birth to what and who we are.

Therein lies the rub. Not all of us, including native people who have acculturated or disconnected from their heritage, think of the earth as home. Sense of place for non-native people does not always include the earth itself—it might be a town, a house, or a birthplace, perhaps, but frequently not the earth. There exists a serious disconnection, and hence no basis for respect, for the natural environment. Some people may fight to have a building declared as a "historic site" for preservation, but they forget the natural environment that was there before the building was constructed. While this may be a harsh charge, that does not preclude it from ringing true. It would not hurt the causes of preservationists to include the earth upon which "historical" buildings sit in their efforts to save and maintain objects of significance to humanity. After all, if the earth is harmed, we all feel the effects.

In the 1950s my grandparents and I had to leave our home on the plateau and move into town. We sold the horses and the wagon, and the log house my grandfather had worked so hard to build. A truck came for the horses one morning, and in the months following that, the man who bought the house dismantled it and hauled it away piece by piece. After a few summers, the prairie reclaimed the site.

Though the house is gone, that plateau is still home, because we had a far greater connection with the land. My memories certainly include the house and the few years of formative childhood I enjoyed there with my grandparents. Now there is only a slight depression in the ground—where the root cellar was—to indicate that people once lived there. And next to the old site are a few bleached bones, all of the physical remains of a good mare. The land is still there, the rolling prairies and deep gullies. Water still seeps out of the ground where the spring was, the dirt long since caved in over the dozens of stones that lined the walls of the well.

Each and every time I walked that plateau, especially after my grandparents died, I was and am reminded that the land has the ability to endure—given an opportunity. That opportunity, however, depends increasingly on humans possessing an awareness of the impact we have on the natural world. That awareness is, I believe, rooted in a sense of place, and if we have a sense of a home that is specific, we could expand the compassion that awareness generates to encompass the entire planet.

PART II

To You We Shall Return

EIGHT: THE ATOMIC AGE

Not until high school history class did I learn that I had been born into the Atomic Age. My imagination and my heart were both firmly rooted in the past, where native warriors fought one another one-on-one and eye-to-eye. Then I read about Hiroshima and Nagasaki in a textbook. Nearly a hundred thousand people—most of them not warriors—died in an instant. That happened only fifteen years before I read about it, and a scant four months before I was born.

Some years after that eye-opening moment, I began to take stock of the world around me. I went home to visit my grandparents and drove them to the plateau where our log house had once stood. They still lived in town and loved to go back to the old place, and so did I. During that visit, I sat on the hill south of the old home site and garden. Beneath a clear sky and a warm autumn sun, I watched a swept-wing B-52 bomber fly over, heading west, probably returning to the air force base at Rapid City.

Since the first single-engine light plane I saw as a boy, I was fascinated with airplanes. I asked how they were able to fly, but my grandfather had no idea, except to say that white people thought of everything. My uncle, in high school at the time, explained that a man sitting in the plane drove it, operating the engine and controls. What the engine and controls were was a mystery to me, until I looked in an encyclopedia much later. As a child growing up on an Indian reservation in the mid 1950s, I experienced many such moments of "discovery." If it was not airplanes, it was electricity, television, or even a cigarette lighter. Matches I knew about, but fire from a little metal box was something else. Of course, most things are a mystery until one dissects them intellectually and literally. Furthermore, my grandfather cautioned that we should not be too impressed with things that we did not completely understand. According to him, if a man could think it up and make it, it was not a miracle, and eventually some other man would figure it out. The question in my six-year-old mind was why white men needed such things as automobiles and electric lights.

At the time most people, Indian or white, likely did not give machines and tools that were part of their everyday lives a second thought. But I did, because I frequently compared them to how my Lakota ancestors lived, and what they used for tools. In the course of their lives, they started fires, butchered animals, cooked, traveled from one place to another, and made clothes. In the 1950s, people bought food and clothing and used whatever appliances and conveniences they could afford to buy. My grandparents and I did not use electricity, though we did have a battery-powered radio. We bought kerosene and white gas to light lamps, and we burned wood for heating and cooking. I never considered that my life was harder or easier because we did not use electricity or because my grandparents did not own an automobile. But my perspective and opinion was limited, based as it was on what I saw in the area in which we lived. I had no idea, of course, of the world that lay beyond the northern part of the Rosebud Reservation.

I only knew that there was a world beyond mine because my uncle had gone to something called a university some distance away. When he joined the army, he first went to a place called Fort Campbell, Kentucky, and then was eventually sent to a place called Korea, to fight in a war (as a second lieutenant with the Eighty-second Airborne). To get there, he had to ride on a big boat that traveled on the water for several days. Though my grandparents did their best to explain these things to me, I had a hard time imagining that there really was a boat so big that many houses the size of ours could fit inside it. Try as I might, I could not visualize what it looked like.

My grandfather also explained that automobiles were faster than horses. He was certain that it would take a horse several days to travel the same distance a car could in one day. Getting from one place to another, I reasoned, was the important thing. Why was it so important to get there faster, or to have large boats or large houses? It was the way of the whites to do these things, my grandparents patiently explained. Why they had those ways and needs was still a mystery to them.

Indeed, much of what white people did was strange, curious, and fascinating, but nonetheless a mystery to me, and probably to most native people. The underlying reason for our contentious relationship with white things and white ways was because in the 1950s, on the Rosebud Reservation and elsewhere, whites were in control.

It was not that native people could go back to buffalo hide lodges, even though many wanted to. Canvas had replaced buffalo hides as the lodge covering for tipis, but it was not as sturdy, as quiet, or as warm in the winter. Canvas lodges rattled in a strong breeze and deteriorated faster than buffalo hide did. The circumstances had changed, and houses made of wood frames or logs were the thing. The Lakota were practical and wise enough to adapt to the circumstances. Though I do recall that neither of my grandparents had any desire to learn how to drive a car. My maternal grandmother never did, because I think she saw driving as capitulation. My paternal grandfather saw it as a necessary thing, no more and no less.

Nonetheless, I was born into an industrialized and mechanized world, and even though the reservation seemed to be at the far end of it, people there used machines and appliances that made life easier. Nevertheless, my generation of Lakota was barely three generations removed from a "primitive" lifestyle. That was not in my awareness as a boy, of course, but looking back as an adult, it is difficult to fully comprehend how times had changed so rapidly.

These thoughts flowed through my mind that day, as they had on many other occasions, as I watched the bomber roaring overhead. But the juxtaposition of a small grassy hill unaffected by human intrusion for thousands and thousands of years, with the symbol of modern man's technological advances flying overhead, is a moment that I still think about frequently. The hill is still there, and except for a barbed-wire fence below it and signs of cattle hoofprints, it is much the same as it always has been, sprouting grass to feed cattle and deer and prairie dogs. The B-52 bomber, of course, has evolved into a version capable of evading radar and delivering death and destruction thousands of miles from its home base. But the question was: Which of those things was I more a part of?

For me, this moment was something of a linchpin regarding time in terms of where I had come from and where I was going. There was no denying my connection to the era in which I lived as a child. My existence was supported by grandparents, who used what was materially at hand to enable us to survive and thrive as a family, much like other Lakota and white families. In that context we were "modern" because we used tables and chairs, beds above the floor, kerosene lamps, iron stoves, and so on. But my grandparents' thinking, their values, and their attitudes were firmly rooted in the past, and those were the aspects of my childhood that influenced me the most. In other words, things—no matter how beneficial or valuable—should not change our identity or influence our values and our character. Several Lakota people, my grandfather among them, put it another way: Adapting to the white man's things and ways does not mean we should adapt to their thinking.

So what was it that so solidly influenced and guided generations of Lakota and their thinking that that they were able to withstand the onslaught of change? I found the answer that day sitting on that hill. It was, and is, the land.

Therefore, though I was born into the Atomic Age, I am not a child of it. I consciously chose to keep and apply the values passed to me by my grandparents.

That does not mean that I reject the world I live in; it simply means that I walk to the beat of a different drummer. The problems I face as a citizen of the world, as an inhabitant of Grandmother Earth, are the same as they are for everyone else, but how I regard them and mitigate them is not the same as everyone else. That does not make me better or wiser—simply different. To state it succinctly, I am a Lakota person governed and guided by Lakota values in a predominantly non-Lakota world.

Having said that, I must also state that the white man's ways are not totally without value. But I do question those ways that affect the natural environment. Might does not make right, and though it can be risky to question anyone or anything in control, we need to, in order to arrive at a consensus regarding what is right and what is wrong. A simple look outside my window reveals the white man's impact on the world I live in now: paved roads, high-line wires, condensation trails across the sky, streetlights piercing the darkness, fences, a neighbor's porch light, and even the small lights that illuminate the walk leading up to my front door. We deem many of those things necessary because they make life easier for us. But we should also have the conscious thought that what is good for man is not necessarily good for the natural environment. That is the legacy of my Lakota ancestors, and it is a marked difference—the beat of a different drummer, the still small voice amid the cacophony of technology and the buzz and hum of modern machines and appliances we use every day. It is a voice we should heed, but just as important, we should understand where it comes from.

It is a voice from the past. How did it come to be, and what gave it substance?

Human beings are that voice: people from the past with hopes and fears, and strengths and weaknesses, who lived their lives in a time and under circumstances that put them in constant, direct contact with the natural environment. Their trials and tribulations, their successes and failures, their experiences and the insights they gained from enduring—and overcoming—adversity is the substance of that voice. The realities they faced every day held the lessons they learned, and those lessons were passed to the next generation and to the next, and so on. But somewhere along the line, the lessons began to fade and lose credibility with succeeding generations. Perhaps we will never know why, but I suspect it has something to do with some form of technology, some tool or machine that gave humans a sense of power. The more power man gained—or the illusion of power—the more disdain he began to have for the land, the trees, the water.

Man assumed dominion, or perhaps it is more accurate to say he assumed that he had dominion. In any case, he functioned from that viewpoint, from that attitude of power. The more trees he felled, the more land he cleared, the more crops he planted, the more animals he domesticated, the more streams he diverted, the more powerful he perceived himself to be and the less connected he felt to anything that was not human or of his making. In one sense, he forgot where he came from. But, sadly, perhaps even tragically, that disconnect was the basis for man soiling his own nest: the earth.

These are realities for me, as much a reality as the computer I used to write this book, the Jeep I drive, the airplanes I frequently travel in, hazardous waste sites, and global warming. The list of realities turns into offenses we modern humans and our industrial-age predecessors have committed against the natural environment: Numerous animal species are extinct, soil and water are contaminated by toxic and nuclear waste, the ozone layer is deteriorating, and the forests are disappearing. Modern man's disconnect with his natural environment is difficult to ignore, and sometimes even more difficult to analyze in terms of what it means for my family and me and for the future of those who come after us—the grandchildren and great-grandchildren.

Many of us reach a point at which we wish for a simpler time—when there was an innocence to it all. Perhaps that wish is the same as a desire to go back to a time before we made the mistakes that led to the vulnerable planet we have today. We have acknowledged that something went wrong, but wonder how those of us who care think the way we do. How do we look back at what we have done to our nest and understand it? Perhaps one way is to go back to the beginning when our species did not perceive itself to be so powerful, when this kind of arrogance did not exist. We can go back to a time when humans realized that they were part of the big picture, not apart from it or above it.

To that end, the pre-European inhabitants of North America are an effective case study if we want an insight into surviving and thriving within the parameters of the natural environment. However, in order to do that we must move beyond our contemporary inclination to regard those societies as archaic. The lessons derived from their lifeways are not necessarily in the size of their structures or villages, or the width of their trails and roads. Rather, we can learn valuable lessons from the materials they used to construct dwellings and where they were located, and why the trails were laid out the way they were.

For me the way to assess the present is to hold it up to the past. It is the standard to which we should hold ourselves—not because our ancestors were infallible or perfect, but because they faced many of the same issues and problems we have today (such as providing food and shelter for our families), and they had to find answers to their problems just as we do today. But such an assessment only works if we know the past and understand that our ancestors are the foundation of our knowledge. They laid the groundwork for our values and beliefs and attitudes, and our faults. Furthermore, they invented many of the tools and apparatuses—or at least the basic versions—that we use today.

But just as we humans are largely unconnected to the natural environment, we are also disconnected from our past. We twenty-first-century humans often seem to consider ourselves the epitome of our species. (It's not a new phenomenon: It was the same in the twentieth century, and in the nineteenth century, too.) We often think we invented everything, good and bad, in the modern era. We simply refuse to understand that it has all been done before, up to and including weapons of mass destruction, ethnocentrism, corrupt governments, colonialism, and the rise and fall of entire nations. Because of that disconnect with our past, we are ignorant to valuable lessons regarding how to do something, as well as how *not* to do something. Perhaps the most grievous sin we have committed is to forget that we all had an intimate relationship with the natural environment at one point in time.

Every modern human society is connected, in one way or another, to ancestors who lived a primitive lifestyle—a lifestyle that was elemental and depended on practical knowledge of the natural, physical environment. The predicament for most nations and societies today is that those beginnings are all but forgotten. Fortunately, there are people who are not as far removed from them, such as we traditional Lakota. This does not mean that every Lakota person alive today can build a fire with a bow drill fire starter, or knows which plants are edible or usable as healing herbs. But enough of us do have some bit of knowledge of that primitive past, and collectively we can offer an insight into a system and a philosophy that regarded Grandmother Earth as a living entity. This is the most important insight we can offer: the benefit of the spiritual connection our ancestors lived by.

A spiritual connection to the natural environment, or at least a respect for it, does not necessarily mean wholesale change for the modern person. Most of us can alter our lifestyle to an extent that is not uncomfortable or unattainable, but that still respects the parameters and needs of the natural environment. Before we can begin to incorporate the ways and means with which to strike an accord with Grandmother Earth, we need to know and understand what the ancient Lakota were about, so we know what to emulate.

I recall a story of an ancestor who was captured by white soldiers nearly 140 years ago. His horse had been injured seriously while scouting for buffalo in late summer, so the young Lakota man was walking home. This was in the area south of where the current town of Mandan, North Dakota, is situated. The soldiers took him north and east, probably toward the settlement of Fort Mandan. The young man realized immediately that his captors had no food, and both the horses and the soldiers were exhausted. They had taken his weapons and his bag of dried meat, which they devoured immediately. Sometime during the second night, he escaped while his captors slept.

Though the young man had no tools or weapons, he managed to survive on various kinds of berries that were at the end of their season, such as chokecherries, vine currants, and buffalo berries. But his staple food was *tinpsila* (timp-see-lah) or wild turnip, a tuber or root vegetable, which he found in abundance.

His biggest worry had been how to escape from the soldiers. After that, survival was not an issue, because he already knew what the land had to offer.

NINE: DRUMS

Drums, for me, represent the connection we Lakota have with Grandmother Earth. But not just any drum. Our drums are made of wood and rawhide and sinew: all natural materials. They are gifts, if you will, from the earth. But the connection is not only the material or the component parts of a drum—it is the beat, the rhythm that emanates from it. Lakota drums sing the heartbeat of the earth.

The drum has an important place in Lakota culture because it is not merely an instrument for entertainment, as musical instruments usually are. It is the primary instrument, the only one, at most social occasions and certainly at all religious and healing ceremonies. It gives voice to the connection of all things in the world. But like all other aspects of Lakota culture as we have known them for the past few hundred years, the drum serves a purpose. It does, in fact, represent the heartbeat of Grandmother Earth.

We Lakota have known since time immemorial that there is a heartbeat to the earth, and we give it voice through the drum. Though some may have forgotten that reality or were duped into believing otherwise, it nonetheless is still a reality. Our ancestors came to understand it long ago and the lifestyles they lived within the parameters of the natural environment for thousands of generations affirmed it again and again.

No one knows for certain where the Lakota originated as a distinct group of people. Non-Lakota historians theorize that we might have come from the southeastern woodlands, and it is possible a part of the nation may have. What we do know for certain is that, for hundreds of years, we have been part of a nation comprised of three main groups: We are the Dakota, Lakota, and Nakota. Before the three groups evolved, we probably did not have those names.

Dakota, Lakota, and Nakota are not only three different groups of people, they are three dialects of a language. The meaning of each name is "allies" or an "alliance of friends." The meanings suggest that separate groups came together to become friends and allies. As dialects, Dakota and Nakota are most similar to each other, while there are notable differences between them and the Lakota dialect. It is possible, therefore, that the Dakota and Nakota people were more closely associated and perhaps were forest dwellers at one time, and that the group that came to be called Lakota came from elsewhere.

Just over three hundred years ago, those three groups made their first contact with Europeans, namely French voyageurs in the lakes region of what is now eastern and northern Minnesota, at the northwestern corner of the Northeast Woodlands culture area. By then the Dakota, Lakota, and Nakota had been in the area for some time and were at odds with other native peoples over territory and resources. Those people who came face-to-face with the French were already part of a highly developed culture, adept at surviving and thriving in their environment.

Whatever circumstances had compelled them to move prior to that, the Dakota and Nakota probably did come from the east, while the Lakota likely traveled south to the lake region from Canada. The three bands knew how to live and thrive in a forest environment, especially one so rich in resources. Food was plentiful in the form of deer, elk, moose, and beaver, and of course a variety of freshwater fish, not to mention an array of fruits, vegetables, and grains, including wild rice. There was a virtually inexhaustible supply of soft and hardwood trees for building dwellings and making tools, weapons, toys, and household furnishings.

Two styles of permanent and semipermanent dwellings were used, now commonly known as wigwams or wikiups. One was made of wood and dome-shaped, a sturdy frame of intersecting poles covered with brush, with an outer covering of birch bark to make it water resistant. This was likely the winter dwelling since it was strong enough to bear the weight of snow. In warmer weather they also used a hide lodge, the small predecessor to the type they would use later on the Plains. This early version was probably made from young pine for the straight support poles for the conical frame and covered with moose, elk, or deer hide. Both types of dwellings were no taller than eight feet and probably twelve to sixteen feet wide at the base. The hide lodge was not as wide. Both were large enough to hold four to six people comfortably, with room for various types of containers for food and clothing, and simple legless chairs. Each had a smoke hole in the top, since an open fire in a dugout pit was used inside for cooking and heating.

These kinds of dwellings were designed and adapted to the forest. They blended in and it was not necessary to clear large trees to set up a village. A village consisted of clusters of lodges interspersed throughout the forest, probably no more than ten in a cluster and no farther than a hundred yards apart. Each cluster of lodges housed about fifty to seventy people with a population comprised of more elders and children than adults in their prime. Therefore a village of five hundred to seven hundred people was artfully blended into the forest, usually arranged in a rough circle, as much as the forest would permit, with the head civilian and military leaders living in the center cluster. All were connected by trails that resembled the spokes of a wheel.

We do not know for certain how long our ancestors lived in the lakes region before the arrival of the French voyageurs. But it was long enough for two separate groups of people to blend into one overall identity, and evolve a language with three separate dialects. Those dialects exist to this day, and the dialect we members of the Dakota, Lakota, and Nakota speak obviously indicates our specific ancestry. Now, as then, we can all understand one another's dialects—given that we speak them, of course.

Interestingly, a term we used to describe a seasonal characteristic of the lakes region is now the state name of Minnesota, which was adapted from the words *mni sota*. *Mni* (mnee) means "water," referring to the hundreds of lakes in the region, and *sota* (sho-tah) means "to mist or smoke." The combined meaning is "misty waters," which occurred when differences in water and air temperatures caused a mist or fog to hang over the lakes. To us, then, the Land of a Thousand Lakes is the Land of Misty Waters.

Whatever circumstances brought our ancestors to that region have long since been forgotten, but one ancient Lakota story offers a clue. Long ago, the people—a common reference used by all native peoples of North America—were living in a country where winter stayed throughout much of the year. They lived by hunting and pursued the great horned deer (probably caribou), which were plentiful. A change in the weather occurred, and for several seasons in a row the deer did not travel their usual trails, and so the people had little food to eat. When the situation became worse, the elders talked about what to do. Eventually a decision was made to send scouts in all directions to see what the situation was like elsewhere. Two of the scouts went south, and after a difficult journey, they found a land of forests and lakes. There, different kinds of deer were plentiful—probably elk, moose, and white-tailed deer. Not only that, there were many kinds of fruits, as well as fish in the lakes. When the two scouts returned with their news, the people decided to move south. It was a difficult trek, but most of them eventually survived the journey and made new homes in the forests among the lakes.

Wherever their homes had been, the people that became the Lakota nation—and also the Dakota and Nakota nations—endured the rigors and dangers of travel to relocate in a different part of the continent. Long distances, the extremes of weather, enemies, and exploring territory new to them were hardships that had to be faced by young and old alike. After they had chosen an area to establish their new villages, they set about living their lives. Unfamiliarity with new territory was the first obstacle, but as a people with a cohesive society, as well as an inherent ability to survive in the natural environment, they were successful in adapting to their new home.

The allied people thrived for several generations because of one significant factor: their willingness and ability to adapt. That enabled them to assess any new environment or situation and ascertain what was necessary to survive within it or with it. For example, they learned to build and use canoes for better access to fish and to turn lakes from obstacles into transportation pathways.

By this point in their societal evolution, they had proven ways and means to ensure their survival. They wasted very little and made every kind of tool and weapon they needed. They lived a sedentary lifestyle in the forest; that is, their villages were more or less permanent. By and large only hunters and scouts traveled great distances to procure food and to keep an eye out for enemies.

If interaction with other people in the lakes region had not become contentious, we might still be living there. As it was, around 1700 the French began trading flintlock rifles to the Anishinabe (Chippewa), who were at odds with my ancestors but did not have the military might to drive them out. With their newfound alliance and increased firepower, the Anishinabe forced the allied people out of the region. The Dakota, Lakota, and Nakota wisely chose not to risk an all-out war, knowing they would suffer serious casualties, causing an immediate impact but many long-term consequences as well. The loss of one man represented the loss of a diverse gene pool. A man's death immediately impacted a community's ability to provide for itself in terms of food and raw materials, since males as hunters did that. Military capability would suffer as well, since males fulfilled the critical role of warriors.

Until the French upset the balance of power, life in the lakes region was good. It was difficult, to say the least, for the Lakota and their relatives to leave. But because their young men had traveled west to hunt, they possessed knowledge of the great open country. Sparsely populated as it was, it was probably the only logical choice for relocation.

Once again, the ability to survive was not an issue. As their great-great-grandparents had done upon arriving in the lakes region, the people had to assess the characteristics of the Plains. The first radically different feature was the lack of trees. There were trees, but only along creeks and rivers. The Plains did not have the thick, endless shady forests the people had grown used to. They were replaced by an endless sea of grass under an open sky unobstructed by tall trees. Sunrises and sunsets were much more evident.

Traveling westward out of the lakes region, the Lakota and their relatives walked onto the eastern edge of the Great Plains, a tall grass prairie. There the land stretched to the horizons as far as the eye could see. They walked, carrying their belongings in packs loaded onto drag poles pulled by dogs. (The horse would not arrive for another generation or two.) They could not bring their dome dwellings, of course, so the shelters they took were the more portable hide lodges. As it turned out, these would be extremely well suited for life on the Plains.

The tall, thigh-high, thick grass, owing to a more-than-adequate rainfall, was the bison's diet, and it became a resource with which the Dakota, Lakota, and Nakota would form a symbiotic relationship with one another and with the bison. More commonly known as buffalo, American bison were not unknown to the Lakota and other forest dwellers. Hunters had traveled to the prairie country and had seen the large, imposing creatures, and some had hunted them.

Owing possibly to their differing origins and preference for a more sedentary lifestyle, the Dakota and Nakota chose to pitch their lodges along the rivers and creeks east of the Great Muddy or Missouri River.

There the topography was predominantly rolling hills, and there were plenty of game animals in addition to the bison. It did not take the two groups long to establish themselves in the tall grass prairie country. Their settlement spanned the area from what is now southwestern Minnesota to southeastern North Dakota, and all of what is now eastern South Dakota south to include northeastern Nebraska.

Meanwhile, the Lakota crossed the Missouri River and headed west across the short grass prairie, where bison proliferated. For 140 years, they would continue to push west until they reached the eastern foothills of the Shining Mountains, or Big Horn Mountains, in what is now central Wyoming. In the process, the Anishinabe pushed aside a small tribe now called the Kiowa, who in turn went south into what is now Nebraska and Kansas. Another group, now known as the Cheyenne, was not as easy to push aside, small in population though they were. The Cheyenne and Lakota eventually formed an alliance that exists to this day.

By the middle of the nineteenth century, the Lakota had become seven separate subgroups, with a population of about twenty thousand people, and controlled a territory bordered on the east at the Missouri River and west at Big Horn Mountains. The northern border was eventually the Yellowstone River, in Montana, and on the south it was the Shell River or North Platte River, which flows into what is now northern Nebraska and southern Wyoming.

Two factors contributed to the growth of the Lakota as people on the prairie: (1) the people's ability and willingness to adapt to life on the northern Plains, and (2) the bison. None of the changes they made were arbitrary. The overall choice they made to cross the Missouri River and take up residence on the great grassy prairies was freely made and it would influence what happened to them thereafter. It was made primarily because of the abundance of bison, the ability to move virtually unimpeded across the open prairies, and their ability to survive in the new environment.

The physical challenge was daunting. Forests could no longer hide clusters of dwellings, and gone were the countless lakes filled with fish. Though the Lakota now had found a seemingly endless resource for food and clothing in the plentiful bison, they had to be hunted, killed, skinned, and butchered, and the meat transported—all on foot. But there was no looking back. On the Plains, the Lakota became nomadic hunters.

Making a living on the Plains was certainly different, if not more difficult. But the worth of a people can be seen in their willingness to accept challenges. The Dakota, Lakota, and Nakota did just that. They did not have to learn how to hunt, but they did have to tailor their approach in the new environment. Hunting in a forest was done either by tracking and stalking, or by sitting in a camouflaged shelter. On the prairie finding the bison was not difficult, because they were easy to track. Yet they were not easy to approach or stalk within the effective range of a bow, which was about forty yards. To ensure a successful kill, the hunter needed to be about twenty yards or closer. Eventually, the Lakota found a unique way to get very close—by hiding in a blind and, at the right moment, ambushing. (The practice of using "buffalo jumps," where a number of animals were driven over a ledge to plunge to their deaths, predated the development of the bow and arrow.)

A blind was simply a pile of brush or a natural thicket or something similar that blended with the immediate environment, something the hunter could hide in or behind. With a blind, the hunter simply waited for an animal or animals to pass close enough to ensure a lethal wound with an arrow. Before long the Lakota, as well as the Dakota and Nakota, adapted hunting techniques to harvest bison. One was to send out scouts year-round to keep abreast of where the various herds were, since their migration patterns changed with the cold weather. Another was the development of the "buffalo lance," which was used primarily during winter hunts. A buffalo lance was probably at least twice as long as the height of a man. After a small herd was chased into extremely deep snow, such as a gully, hunters on snowshoes approached close enough to kill the bison by piercing them through the heart with the lance.

After closely observing the interaction between bison and wolves, the Lakota and other Plains tribes noticed that one or two wolves were not a dire threat to a herd, so the wolves could approach fairly close without alarming them. Taking that lesson, Lakota hunters wearing a wolf hide and/or wolf headdress mimicked the movements of wolves and crawled close enough to a herd to loose a few arrows, and then crawled away.

Hunting was not a seasonal sport. It was the way to make a living all year round, the primary way to procure food and materials for clothing and shelter. Therefore, after migrating to a new environment, the Lakota ensured that their methods and weapons were equal to the responsibility. Innovations to techniques, as well as improvements or redesign of weaponry, were critical to the welfare of the entire community. This did not mean, however, that other aspects of Lakota life and society were not important or were unaffected by innovation.

Once on the virtually treeless prairies west of the Missouri, the nomadic lifestyle might have been unavoidable—it probably was possible to establish permanent villages—but given that the food sources moved about freely over vast distances, it was prudent to go with the flow. Furthermore, a permanent village meant that women, children, and the elderly would be left largely unprotected while men were away hunting for days at a time.

After several generations as sedentary forest dwellers in what is now Minnesota, the Lakota did not consider ways to alter the environment to suit their needs. They simply adapted. It is what people do when they respect and understand Grandmother Earth.

That ability to adapt brings me back to the concept of the drum as the connector of our people to the earth. Listening to a Lakota drum and watching dancers in a circular arena represents, for me, balance. We Lakota, at least in that arena, dance to the heartbeat of Grandmother Earth. Hundreds of years ago our ancestors migrated to the northern Plains and learned to survive in a difficult, even harsh and unforgiving environment where others had not. They survived because they did not fight the environment. They survived because they understood the realities of it and accepted the limitations it placed on them. Within that balance, they became a strong people.

That is what the drum reminds us of. But there is more to the story.

TEN: AWAY FROM THE VILLAGE

The Great Plains occupies the center of the northern tier of the North American continent. Using today's map, it stretches from what is now Texas to the Canadian province of Alberta. It encompasses the entirety of four states and varying portions of seven other states and two other Canadian provinces. On the east it is tall grass prairie, and on the west it is short grass prairie, thanks to up to forty and twenty inches of rain per year, respectively. To understand this vast stretch of prairie is to gain an insight into the cultures of the indigenous peoples who inhabited it, as many as sixty different tribes or nations.

Overwhelmingly, most of the tribes who occupied the Plains were nomads. Their predominant method of procuring food and other raw materials was by hunting, which they did almost constantly. Food was the basic necessity, but large ungulates—hoofed animals such as deer, elk, antelope, bighorn sheep, and bison—were also the sources of materials for clothing, robes, and shelter. Bison became the main resource because of their size—each weighing almost a ton—and their sheer numbers, estimated to be in the millions. They were the primary source for a variety of items used in everyday life: Their furry hides were used for rugs, blankets, and ceremonial robes. But the scraped hides were most prized as coverings for the conical lodges used by many different tribes. Several hides, scraped of hair, were trimmed and sewn together to form the half moon–shaped lodge coverings. The hides were thick enough to stop cold winter winds, and, when thoroughly smoked, were even water resistant. In addition to the hides, the bison's bones, hooves, hair, sinew, and horns were used to make tools, weapons, utensils, ropes, toys, thread and string, drinking cups, spoons, glue, and ceremonial bells, among other things.

Smaller ungulates such as deer, elk, and bighorn sheep were also the source for many of the same products derived from the bison, but they were the main source of materials for clothing and a few household items, such as containers for clothing and food.

So the people followed those animals, moving their villages several times a year. There were a few exceptions to that lifestyle; the Mandan along the Upper Missouri River region lived in permanent earthen lodges in permanent villages. On the southern Plains, the Osage and the Pawnee lived in earth lodges as well, for part of the year.

There were, of course, those people who came to the Plains, saw the lay of the land, and left. Perhaps they considered it too vast, or too cold, or too hot. Perhaps the sheer size of it was too intimidating. Or perhaps after one winter or two of being pushed around by howling winds and chilled to the bone by subzero temperatures, they left for warmer, gentler climes. If that did not chase them away, perhaps it was the oppressive, late-summer heat that sometimes made it difficult for man or beast to breathe.

There were many who stayed and were the stronger for it. The land either taught them to endure or it drove them away. Like indigenous people anywhere on the continent, the people of the Plains not only derived their living from the land—they were also forged by it.

Non-native observers from time to time have characterized native peoples as the original environmentalists. To use such a label sets the natural world apart from whatever man perceives himself to be. In the minds of most, if not all, of the indigenous people of North America, there was no such distinction. The environment was all one thing, and humans were part of it. Therefore, it was not necessary to have a set of practices designed specifically for the environment. Humans simply lived and moved sensibly and respectfully within it, and many people regarded doing so as a responsibility, even a sacred obligation. Such an approach thereby kept their impact to a minimum. Whatever signs of their presence were left behind were absorbed or erased by the earth in a short span of time.

Interestingly, in the Lakota language there is no word for *wilderness*. The word *manitu* (mah-nee-doo) has, at the insistence of non-native scholars and linguists, been "adapted" to mean wilderness. However, its true meaning is simply "away from the village," meaning logically where the people were not. Suffice it to say, if there was not a word to specify "wilderness," there was not then a concept of it. The environment was the environment, and it was all-inclusive.

On the other hand, perhaps there is some logic in regarding indigenous people on this continent as the original environmentalists, if for no other reason than they respected it. But even more than that—they loved it. The Winnebago, a small tribe that lived along the Missouri River in the area where the three states of South Dakota, Nebraska, and Iowa now come together, have a saying:

> *Holy Mother Earth, the trees and all nature are witnesses of your thoughts and deeds.*

Such a sentiment does not suddenly pop into someone's mind; it evolves over time, ruminating in the hearts and souls of people who have lived close to the earth for a long, long time. Such a sentiment rises out of the love for Grandmother Earth.

⌗

I recall that my grandmother had a few favorite spots along the Little White River. In the summers she would ask my grandfather to stop the wagon so that we could sit in the shade of huge cottonwoods and have a meal. The two of them loved to sit and listen to the river, and the breeze rustling in the cottonwood leaves. They watched whatever happened around us, whether it was the breeze swaying the shrubs and grasses or cottontail rabbits scurrying through the brush. On hot days we would cool off by wading in the river, or by sitting on the bank to dip our feet in the cool current. I can therefore say of both of my grandparents, *they were of the earth*.

I never heard either of my grandparents complain about the land. Never did I hear them say that a slope was too long, the river was too deep or wide, or the grass too tall. They would say such things as a matter of fact: there was too little rain, or the snow was deep, or some other fact that we would have to live with or take into account. Never did they blame the earth for any problem or difficulty we had to face. It was not the earth's fault or doing if we were not careful enough to avoid a slope where a slide was likely to occur, or if we were careless enough to linger in a gully during a hard rain, or if we were foolish enough to consider crossing the river in a dangerous spot where the current was too strong. The earth was the way it was and did what it did. It was up to us to learn about it, to understand it, and to take the consequences of ignoring its realities. This was all part of respecting Grandmother Earth.

They told me stories of elderly people in the past leaving the village and their families and returning to a favorite place to die. Most people today would find that appalling or even think it "uncivilized." But to my grandparents it was the epitome of respect for two realities in life. One was death, the ultimate reality, and the other was returning to the earth after we live our lives. Therefore, old men or women, realizing they were too ill or too infirm with age and a burden to their families, would choose to die in a place they were fond of for some reason. Perhaps it was a small brook in a shady glen, or a particular hillside that overlooked a river valley, or a hill that provided a panoramic view of the prairies all around. To them it was a place of cherished memory, and therefore a place of peace—a place where they wanted to have their final view of Grandmother Earth, while they were still on this side and could choose.

Places and landmarks were obviously important to people individually and as a community. N. Scott Momaday, the Pulitzer Prize–winning author and a member of the Kiowa nation, spoke of that custom vividly when he described going to his grandmother's grave, in his book *The Road to Rainy Mountain*:

> *A single knoll rises out of the plain in Oklahoma, north and west of the Wichita Range. For my people, the Kiowa, it is an old landmark, and they gave it the name Rainy Mountain. The hardest weather in the world is there. Winter brings blizzards, hot tornadic winds arise in the spring, and in the summer the prairie is an anvil's edge. The grass turns brittle and brown, and it cracks beneath your feet. There are green belts along the river and creeks, linear groves of hickory and pecan, willow and witch hazel. At a distance in July or August the steaming foliage seems almost to writhe in fire. Great green and yellow grasshoppers are everywhere in the tall grass, popping up like corn to sting flesh, and tortoises crawl about on the red earth, going nowhere in the plenty of time. Loneliness is an aspect of the land. All things in the plain are isolated; there is no confusion of objects in the eye, but* one *hill or* one *tree or* one *man. To look upon that landscape in the early morning, with the sun at your back, is to lose the sense of proportion. Your imagination comes to life, and this, you think, is where Creation was begun.*

Momaday captured the Lakota sentiment for Paha Sapa, or the Black Hills, the only mountain formation on the Plains. The Hills are unique in that there is only one other mountain formation in the world, in New Zealand, that is similar. Not only are they beautiful, they are the very symbol of the spiritual connection the Lakota had, and have, with Grandmother Earth. It is referred to as "the heart of all things" and the "center of the world." Interestingly, it was the geographic center of the territory that the Dakota, Lakota, and Nakota people controlled by the middle of the 1850s. But perhaps even more interesting is the startling fact that photographs taken from space show the Black Hills to be formed in the shape of a human heart.

So the Great Plains not only taught the people how to live, how to be strong and endure, and how to be good people—it endeared itself to them. But it also gave them everything they needed to live and prosper and thrive. It is no wonder then, that at the very least, the people respected the earth. Nor is it surprising that they loved the earth.

I recall particularly how much my grandmother delighted in seeing the first buds on tree branches in the spring, which meant that leaves would soon sprout. She took the same delight in seeing the first little green berries on the chokecherry shrubs, or buffalo berry bushes. As a mother she could identify with new life growing. With those memories, it is not difficult at all for me to visualize her mother, her grandmother, and great-grandmother feeling exactly the same way. While I did not live the same lifestyle as my great-grandparents, I did see their respect and love for the land, their connection to it in my grandmother's eyes. I heard it in her voice as she uttered her joy over new life each spring.

All of these are positive realities, but there are—and were—those that were not: droughts, floods, deep snow, winters so cold it was dangerous to breathe outside the lodge, prairie fires started by lightning, swarms of grasshoppers, tornados, hailstones as large as birds' eggs, and so on. The only answer to avoiding and surviving those harsh and often life-threatening situations is to be seasonally aware of the conditions that are the cause. Knowing will not prevent disasters, such as a drought, from happening, but it will provide an opportunity to avoid problems, as well as to take people out of harm's way.

One of my grandmothers, my maternal grandmother's aunt, told a story one evening of how she and her mother crawled into a dense chokecherry thicket and survived a tornado. (This had to have occurred around 1882.) Her mother had been watching the clouds form all afternoon, and when the storm was imminent, she took her children to a creek bottom filled with chokecherry shrubs. She chose the thickest, densest one and made everyone crawl in. The storm came, and then the twister. It knocked over large cottonwood trees and uprooted other trees. Though frightened out of their wits, my grandmother, her sister, and their mother clung to the stalks of chokecherry bushes as the tornado roared and hurled debris through the creek bottom. The chokecherry stalks bent with the wind—almost down to the ground—because they were flexible hardwood, but they did not break like larger trees did. My ancestor had saved her children and herself because of a simple bit of knowledge, either passed down to her or learned firsthand. Such was life on the Plains.

One can look at a map of North America that delineates the indigenous culture areas and see that the Plains are the second-largest culture area. But such a map does not reveal the character of the land, the natural environment. There is nothing to indicate its cycles, rhythms, and patterns. That knowledge, that sort of intimate connection, is the reward for living on and with the land, from being pushed to your human limits and, in the end, learning that man will never really "tame" or "conquer" it. That flimsy delusion comes from building a road or a bridge and thinking you've significantly changed the laws of nature. We humans suffer from the delusion of power when it comes to the natural environment. In the end it will outlive us all. But even the arrival of the horse on the Plains did not fool the Lakota into thinking they were any more powerful compared with Grandmother Earth. Even when the horse changed everything.

The horse probably arrived—by trade or by other means of acquisition—on the Plains just before 1700. Contrary to what many non-native historians have assumed, the horse did not create the nomadic cultures of the Plains. Such an assumption is a poorly disguised way of taking credit for the "great horse cultures" that seemed to suddenly flourish. Most of the Plains tribes were nomadic before the coming of the horse and were even more so after its arrival. Its impact was tremendous and brought many changes, some of them more obvious than others.

One not-so-obvious effect manifested itself in the size of bison hide dwellings. Before the horse, the dog was the beast of burden for nomadic people, and even the largest dog could only carry half of a lodge covering that stood about eight to ten feet high. After the horse came, the design and configuration of the lodge did not change, but its size did, simply because the horse could carry much larger loads on drag poles. The hide dwelling became taller: from twelve to eighteen feet high, and just as wide across its base. A lodge twelve feet wide across its floor was usually twelve feet high, so of course the support poles increased in number and size. An eighteen-foot-high lodge would have poles as long as twenty-six feet, for example. But the impact of the horse on the lodge did not end there. There was another, more significant consequence.

An increase in space in the lodge made more room for families, an increase of an average of two or three people. Horses could carry home more fresh meat from the hunt. By the middle of the nineteenth century, the Lakota population grew to between fifteen thousand and twenty thousand.

A more obvious effect of the arrival of the horse was that a larger population meant a need for more raw materials. That caused tribes with larger populations to expand the size of the territory they controlled. On the northern Plains, the Lakota were the most populous group and eventually controlled a large area.

The horse precipitated perhaps the most common and enduring image of indigenous people: that of the horse-mounted, lance-wielding warrior wearing a feather bonnet. That image obscures the varied cultures that existed prior to the horse, and perhaps even suggests that indigenous people were nothing without it. We should remember that the era of the horse spanned about 150 years, and indigenous North Americans had survived and thrived without it for well over ten thousand years.

No doubt the horse enhanced indigenous cultures. But did it make indigenous people better—as in more intelligent, more moral, or more ethical? Of course not. Cultural values and norms were well in place before the horse ever appeared on the Plains. (Militarily, the horse did turn many Plains tribes into exceedingly skilled and effective light cavalry, as noted by European nobility and military officers who happened to visit and make their comparisons to European cavalry.)

Nor did the horse change the indigenous people's attitude toward the natural environment. The horse brought with it the ability for our people to move farther and faster, and as such was an invaluable resource. However, being a more productive hunter or warrior was not exclusively because of the horse or the hunter or the warrior. The horse did not necessarily increase fighting skills or encourage devotion to duty. It was simply a means and a platform for the warrior to more effectively defend and protect his people. Indigenous people did not assume a loftier attitude toward the earth just because the horse gave them more options or made them more successful.

In the years after my grandfather sold his horses and wagon, we walked, because we had no other form of transportation. My maternal grandparents moved into town after I had gone to live with my paternal grandparents in order to start school, which began with kindergarten at the age of eight. Not until years later did I wonder why I had to go and live with my paternal grandparents. Obviously I was never part of the discussions that went on between the two sets of grandparents, but the primary concern had been that–at the age of seven–I was not yet in school. In the summer of 1954 I was essentially given back to my maternal grandparents because, by the time I was ready for second grade, they had moved to town, and our house was five blocks from the school.

During those formative years, I saw my parents only occasionally, since they had to go where the work was, from one farm or ranch to another. As far as I understand, my maternal grandparents had insisted on raising me—their first grandchild—and I was taken to live with them before my first birthday. Whatever the circumstances that had brought this arrangement about, it was the most profound thing that has ever happened to me. But in a few years, I returned to live with the people who had raised me and gave me the foundation for who I am.

When we walked, one of them would point to an area or a landmark I knew nothing about, and tell me how it was something significant. Neither one told me never to forget what they were telling me, but I knew even then that I was being given that responsibility—a duty, if you will—not to forget. It was the way to continue their, and our people's, connection to the land. Even as a small child I somehow sensed that it was necessary to listen when either of my grandparents, or any other elder, had a story to tell. Perhaps it was that intrinsic connection between grandparent and grandchild. In any case, I knew that my part of that particular connection was to stay quiet and listen. By staying quiet, one opens oneself to a gift of words and images that can end up as immeasurably beneficial and rewarding.

I have stumbled about in jungles, watched heat shimmer like glass over desert sands, marveled at snow-capped peaks in the Altai Mountains in central Siberia, and listened to waves of three different oceans wash ashore. But as pleasing as those vistas and experiences were to my senses and to my spirit, I always felt best at home. I always thought of the grassy prairies that stretched away from me, the hazy swath of distant hills against the morning sky. I am, after all, a child of the Plains, and I have never and will never forget that connection.

ELEVEN: IF ONLY THE LAND COULD TALK

A simple statement is sometimes like a one-dimensional map: It provides very little information. For example, to say that some of the indigenous people of North America were sedentary and some were nomadic provides only superficial data. It does not begin to provide an insight into how either the sedentary or nomadic peoples lived.

Someone once wrote that in pre-European days, a squirrel could climb up a tree in what is now Florida and travel all the way to east Texas without setting foot on the ground. That either means a lot of trees stood in a straight line across half the continent, or that the forests were exceedingly thick. There was plenty of everything, an abundance, before the Europeans came, trees included. So it probably was possible for a wandering squirrel to get from the eastern end of the continent to the middle by staying in the treetops. But while squirrels could travel unimpeded in a forest, people on the ground could not. So, for sedentary societies, living and thriving in forests was not an arbitrary choice. Therefore, those indigenous groups who came to the forest realized immediately that establishing permanent villages was the only way to live—or at least the easiest. Permanent villages meant permanent dwellings, and an abundance of trees meant those dwellings were constructed of wood. And because dwellings built of sturdy logs could bear more weight, a second floor was added, as well as separate family compartments.

Most of the indigenous societies living in the Eastern Woodlands had permanent villages and dwellings made of wood. Among several tribes, such as those composing the Haudenosaunee (Iroquois) and Wyandot (Huron), they were known as longhouses. The Lenape (Delaware) and Mahican also sometimes used them. As the name suggests, they were about sixty feet long by up to twenty feet wide, and were used communally. That is, several families lived in one dwelling. Their construction was basically post and beam, with bent saplings supporting the roof. Covering was mostly large, rectangular slabs of bark, usually elm.

People living in the pine forests along the Northwest Coast had dwellings of similar design, called plank houses. They were also rectangular in shape and about thirty feet wide by sixty feet long. These homes were made of hand-split logs shaped into planks and tied together vertically or horizontally to a post-and-beam frame. Like the longhouses, plank houses housed several families.

But perhaps the most iconic dwellings, other than the Plains bison hide tipis were the cliff dwellings and pueblos of the southwest and the snow igloos of the Arctic and Subarctic regions. Both are the epitome of the practice of making the best possible use of available materials.

The topography of the Southwest culture area varies from plateaus and mesas to deep canyons and deserts. It is a dry region with less than twenty inches of average annual rainfall. Plants and trees include mesquite, shrub cactus, evergreens, piñon, and juniper—nothing that could be used for family dwellings. So the people who lived there used stone and adobe bricks, the latter made of clay and grass or straw. With stone and adobe bricks, they built homes, some of which still stand but date back hundreds of years. (In fact, the Acoma pueblo is the oldest continuously occupied community in the United States, dating back to the twelfth century.) We look at the ruins of cliff dwellings or other adobe structures and wonder how anyone could live in such a desolate place. Where was the food? Game was not as plentiful here as it was in other parts of the continent. So some of those ancient people became farmers, developing skills to raise crops, enough to feed hundreds of people living in permanent desert villages. They used what little water there was to the best advantage, some developing gravity irrigation techniques.

Whether or not the desert tribes chose to live here is not as significant as the fact that they managed to survive. Those who did not farm hunted, gathered berries and nuts, and dug for edible roots. And those people who did not live in adobe structures or cliff dwellings built small huts, pole frames covered with brush and soil, or hogans, a cone-shaped structure of logs with stick siding covered with mud or sod.

Far to the north, another part of the continent was, and is, far more desolate. It is a place where snow, ice, and cold temperatures stay around for most of the year. So we wonder again, who would willingly choose to live in such a place? The answer is obvious: tough and resourceful people.

In the Arctic and Subarctic regions, winters long and severe, there are only a few hours of daylight. For a number of days, the sun stays below the horizon north of the Arctic Circle. Cold, snow, ice, gale-force winds, and dimly lighted days make human survival doubtful, not to mention that only seals, whales, and caribou are the primary sources of meat. But obviously there were sufficient numbers to sustain a human population, and like indigenous people anywhere on the continent, the Arctic and Subarctic tribes made maximum use of animals taken in a hunt. Hunting is rarely easy, but pursuing whales on the open ocean in skin boats and while armed with stone-tipped harpoons takes particularly precise physical skill, as well as courage. In terms of difficulty, that is certainly in the realm of a mounted hunter chasing a galloping bison across the prairies.

In regions where winter is the predominant season, it also takes a certain amount of physical fortitude just to live. But the people of the north did live there, in dwellings made of ice and snow. Dwellings were made of other materials, to be sure, but the idea of sleeping beneath a dome of ice does not exactly induce a feeling of comfort for most people. Nevertheless, the people who called this region home were quite comfortable. Furthermore, if the stories of entire communities living beneath deep winter snow, their igloos connected by tunnels, for two to three months of the year are true, then that is a yet another stellar example of people adapting to their environment.

Winter nights that last for months, temperatures dipping to –80°F, and hungry polar bears are formidable dangers to contend with. But they were part of the reality of life in the Arctic. Yet another amazing reality is that indigenous people did live and thrive there. Their descendants, with the highest percentage of indigenous descendants remaining in ancestral territory, still live there.

Of course, if we could have conversations with indigenous people who lived in other parts of the continent, there would be as many opinions of what was more dangerous or more beautiful. The people who lived in what is now Florida and along its Gulf Coast would certainly say that alligators, crocodiles, swamps, and poisonous snakes were nothing to take lightly. Those who lived in the mountains of what is now Montana or Utah would likely try to convince us that there are very few natural occurrences that have the sheer power to rival an avalanche of snow.

In short, life was not easy anywhere. Every place and region had its share of beauty as well as danger. And danger was not always obvious, and could be as innocuous as moss on a stone causing a foot to slip and fall into an icy stream—or an alligator floating just beneath the surface of a scummy pond, or a polar bear hidden by blowing snow, or poisonous mushrooms growing among the edible varieties. How about the searing heat of the desert, with a scorpion no bigger than a quarter hidden under a leaf; a coastal hurricane; thin river ice; a sudden blizzard; blinding sandstorms; flash floods; prairie and forest fires; heavy jungle humidity; an angry moose or a swarm of hornets. The list of dangers to be found in nature could go on and on indefinitely.

Without a doubt, there were casualties. People suffered injuries and died from a variety of causes. Not all injuries or deaths could be prevented, but among the significant reasons they occurred were accidents, carelessness, recklessness, homicide, and warfare. The basic difference between life and death was knowledge and common sense—and now and then a lucky break. It is difficult to know definitively the leading cause for fatalities, but hunting in its various forms is a leading contender because it was a constant activity. There are numerous stories from different tribes about men who went hunting and never came home. There are many ways in which men could have died while hunting, ranging from exposure to bad weather to carelessness.

This was one of the reasons expectant mothers wished and prayed to have sons: Men were sorely needed as hunters and primary providers, and highly valued in their communities. Everyone was valued in a community, but adult males procured food and the raw materials for just about everything essential: clothing, shelter, and security. Thus, when a man did not come home, the family and community lost a son, a father and probably a grandfather, a husband, a hunter, a warrior, and likely a community leader. The loss of a single man left a large void. I remember my grandfather leaving food or tobacco offerings on the prairie, on some hill, or along the river, in remembrance. His sentiment was that we would never know who might have passed this way long ago. But he seemed to feel that someone had, or that someone had died in some particular place. "Maybe it was some humble man trying to feed his family," he would say.

It is also difficult to know what the indigenous population of North America was at any given time. Non-native archeologists and anthropologists often advance estimates ranging from three to ten million. Such guesses and theories are somewhat unimportant to native people today. The incontestable fact that our ancestors were here first is immeasurably more important. Furthermore, they lived and thrived in every part of this continent. "I came, I saw, I conquered," Caesar may have written, but from an indigenous North American perspective, that is the creed of arrogance, the edict of a conqueror, the condescending mind-set of a colonizer. Our indigenous ancestors operated from a different viewpoint. They came, they saw, they adapted. They learned their lessons, they took their losses, and—for the most part—they persevered.

I say *for the most part* because not all indigenous societies and groups survived. Some disappeared or died out for any number of reasons before the Europeans arrived. They fell by the wayside owing to bad luck, starvation, extreme weather, or climactic conditions, or perhaps they were just not as strong.

> *What is life? It is the flash of a firefly in the night. It is the breath of a buffalo in the winter time. It is the little shadow which runs across the grass and loses itself in the sunset.*

These are the dying words of Crowfoot, a Blackfoot leader, spoken in 1890, thirteen years after he unwillingly relinquished forty thousand acres of land to the Canadian government. It is said that he might have been referring to the loss of the bison. [*Touch the Earth: A Self-Portrait of Indian Existence*, 1971].

Though the lives of our ancestors as individuals are over, their legacies as nations and societies live through their descendants. Those who survived were either tough as nails or very lucky. Sadly, we will never know exactly who those lost ones were, those who died out and left nothing behind. They may be only shadows that run across our memories, but we will never forget that they were here, too.

Many people, my grandfather included, often said, "If only the land could talk." Indeed. The stories would probably overwhelm us. They would fill in the blanks left by maps and cold scholarly pronouncements. They would obliterate theories, or perhaps prove them, and give another dimension to artifacts left buried.

Several years ago a man I met proudly showed me his collection of projectile points, nearly two dozen stone points made of obsidian and flint discovered in Wyoming and South Dakota. The glass that covered the shadow box case had several cracks. The man said he had already replaced the glass several times. Each time it would eventually crack again. He blamed it on a tight fit because the glass cutter had continued to measure it improperly. But I had a different feeling regarding the cracks.

Those stone points were old, probably thousands of years old, and given that each was found at a different place, each was crafted by a different person. Therefore, that collection of stone projectile points was a direct connection to nearly two dozen highly skilled craftsmen. Since each of them was exquisitely made, they were all probably mature individuals: men who had crafted stone points all of their lives. As far as I was concerned, it was their energy, some vestige of their humanity, if you will, that cracked the glass in defiance of the confinement—as if someone was saying that there were stories there, wanting to be set free. If only we knew how to listen.

Somewhere in my mind I can see one of those brown-skinned flintknappers sitting by a low fire beneath a tree. He is holding a fist-sized piece of obsidian (volcanic glass), carefully studying the direction of the grain in the rock. Then he strikes off a flake from the obsidian using a hammer stone, or with the base of an antler. Then he shapes the flake with the tip of an antler tine. He continues fashioning the point as, ever alert, he keeps an eye out for intruders. Neither young, nor old, he works, pushing at the edges of the flake, wasting no motion. Holding the emerging point to the sky, he assesses his handiwork with a shrewd, knowing gaze.

Along the same lines, a recent television documentary about modern Iñupiaq people near Barrow, Alaska, depicted them hunting a bowhead whale in 2008. A tangential story in the documentary revealed that, some years earlier, a bowhead had been killed in the waters off Barrow. When it was butchered, a stone harpoon point was found lodged inside the carcass. Considering the life span of bowheads, that point was likely around 150 years old. Depending on the migratory habits of that whale, that point—nearly the size of a man's palm—could have been made by any one of the whale-hunting tribes living along the coast, from Alaska to Washington.

Unfortunately, the land may not talk in a literal sense, but it still gives us clues about its history and those who've come before us. We modern humans by and large want tangible proof before we believe. "Seeing is believing" is the axiom by which we abide. Consequently, it is not surprising that non-native historians are still not totally convinced that native oral tradition is a reliable source for historical information, which is a tacit endorsement of the idea that written history is infallible. Neither oral nor written history is infallible, of course. All sources of historical information and data must be closely examined until proven or disproved. So where do pictographs (prehistoric drawings) and petroglyphs (prehistoric carvings) fit in this discussion, relative to North America? For that matter, what of the numerous mounds, such as the Cahokia Mounds near St. Louis, which were built long before Europeans arrived?

It can and has been argued that pictographs and petroglyphs cannot and do not represent a complete story, which is basically true because all the factors relative to their creation are not known. We can guess which group of indigenous people was living in a particular region where pictographs or petroglyphs are located, and sometimes we know with reasonable certainty. But what we do not know is who exactly painted or carved pictures inside a cave or on a rock wall. We will never know. Even if that person left a signature, we would not know it. But there is a wealth of information that cannot be disputed, such as evidence of activities, clothing or ceremonial dress, weapons, tools, game animals, and dwellings. All offer an invaluable glimpse into the lifestyle of the people represented by the artist or artists who painted the pictographs or carved the petroglyphs.

For instance, we can discern a hunting scene, with hunters wielding weapons from atlatls to bows and arrows, and pursuing animals from mammoths to mountain goats. Looking at a pictograph or a petroglyph brings to mind what my grandfather liked to say: "Someone passed this way." It also points to the most significant indisputable reality of all: indigenous people were here thousands and thousands of years ago. They were our ancestors, those who showed us the way. And they knew generations of descendants would follow them. So they painted pictures of their lives because they did not want to be forgotten. Yet paintings and rock carvings were not all that was left behind.

Sometime in the nineteenth century came the first Euro-American discoveries of earthen mounds, primarily along or east of the Mississippi River Valley. Though they were obviously man-made, the immediate assumption was that they could not have been the work of indigenous people, and were attributed to lost

European tribes. Once that narrow-minded view was cast aside, scholars realized what a cultural treasure trove the mounds were. But what exactly were earthen mounds?

For the most part they were for either burial or ceremonial purposes. Some were built in the shape of animals, such as the Serpent Mound in Ohio. As the name suggests, it is in the shape of a long, uncoiling serpent. Mounds varied in size and shape. Some were only a few feet high. A mound at Poverty Point, one of the oldest sites in present-day northeast Louisiana stands seventy feet high, and is 640 feet long by 700 feet wide. Archeologists think this and the other mounds at this site were probably constructed between 1800 and 500 BC. But perhaps the largest site is the Cahokia Mounds in Illinois, near St. Louis. It originally covered four thousand acres and contained more than eighty burial and temple mounds. One, known as Monks Mound, stands a hundred feet high and covers sixteen acres.

In the company of two friends, I visited the Cahokia site on a cool, rainy day in the spring of 2009. The rain prevented us from doing the walking tour, but the life-sized dioramas in the museum took us back a thousand years. Cahokia was a complex society built on trade, and was a thriving city of thousands with earthen mounds whose size rivaled the largest Mayan and Aztec temples. Many of the mounds have been destroyed, the soil hauled away and used in construction projects in the area. But, like pictographs and petroglyphs and stone projectile points, those mounds that remain—adorned with climbing stairs for tourists—are a tangible sign from the past. Strangely, but perhaps somehow appropriately, the low-hanging rain clouds obscured the surrounding modern landscape, isolating the site as if trying to transport it back to another time.

⧺

There are always a variety of emotions present during such experiences, and there certainly were for me, as a native person, on that brief visit to the Cahokia site. The people who lived there about a thousand years ago were culturally different from my direct ancestors, but it is gratifying and empowering to know that people like me created Cahokia.

Tragically, the Cahokian culture suffered a decline for reasons we will never truly know. But that, too, is a heritage that all present-day indigenous peoples of North America share. Yet before we react angrily or sadly to that fact, let us remind ourselves of all the cultures and societies the world over that have risen and fallen over the millennia, as well as those that are currently in decline. A legacy that is far more valid an example for us to emulate is that our indigenous ancestors came to terms with their environment: They thrived with it and within it. That is the reality that hides behind anglicized versions of indigenous names on maps, and terms such as *nomadic*, *sedentary*, and *hunter-gatherers*. Rest assured, there is much more than meets the eye.

TWELVE: THE INVENTION OF THE ARROW

We all know the axiom "Whatever does not kill you will make you stronger," and most of us can identify with it and we probably have an experience that symbolizes it for us: Marine Corps boot camp, for example; a marathon; the stairs leading up to a walk-up flat on the seventeenth floor; or dealing with a work supervisor whose charm rivals that of Attila the Hun. But in a real sense, that kind of an experience can help us understand how the various indigenous cultures of pre-European North America developed a spiritual connection to the natural environment.

Sometime in our ancient past, humans had to have realized that fighting against or controlling the natural environment was not possible. That did not stop humans from affecting the environment to some extent to ensure their own survival and comfort. They cut down trees and harvested other natural materials to build shelters.

They planted seeds, they built crude bridges over creeks or narrow chasms, diverted streams for irrigation, and accomplished other rudimentary feats of engineering. Perhaps five or six thousand years ago in North or South America, indigenous people experimented with cross-breeding different types of grasses and eventually produced maize—the forerunner of corn.

Not only did corn become an important food crop, it was also a valuable medium of trade. Obviously the agrarian lifestyle, instigated by corn and other food crops such as pumpkins and squash, necessitated the clearing of land for planting. The construction of burial and temple mounds discussed in the previous chapter certainly affected the environment, since thousands of tons of soil were dug and transported and piled. All across the continent, as primitive societies increased in population, the more they harvested raw materials from the natural environment, be it trees for tools or weapons or building materials, mud and rock from streams, fruits and vegetables, or the quarrying of various types of stone for knives and projectile points. In short, primitive indigenous people in North America did have an impact on the natural environment. Though that impact was not negligible, they did not deplete species of plants or animals to the point of near extinction, or intentionally pollute the rivers to the point where the water became undrinkable.

A custom among several northern Plains tribes is an indicator that indigenous people before the nineteenth century were indeed aware of their impact on the natural environment, and regarded the earth as something more than a supply source. Hunters left offerings after killing animals, usually a bundle of tobacco or prairie sage. Some verbally gave thanks and then asked for forgiveness from the animal. As a matter of fact, indigenous people everywhere had similar traditions and practices. Modern-day Iñupiaq whale hunters pray after killing a bowhead whale, giving thanks to God and the whale. One hunter spoke of how the whale was a gift from God and that they were able to harvest it because the whale "gave itself" to the hunters.

Hand in hand with offering thanksgiving, hunters actually humbled themselves in the presence of the dead animal, taking a moment to honor the life they had taken.

Such traditions of preparation and thanksgiving were not restricted to animals. Gifts were offered in return for many things taken or harvested from the land. When a Lakota bow maker cut a tree that would become a bow, he too left an offering. He also might pray before cutting the tree, asking for the privilege of taking it. He knew and understood that the tree was a living entity with just as much right to life as any form of life on the earth. That knowledge and understanding arose out of the realization that life was *the* common reality. Anything and everything that was alive was connected to all else that was alive. That was the connection, the unavoidable reality. The common denominators were birth and death. All living things come into the world, whether we hatch from eggs, grow from seeds, or emerge from the womb. And in the end, after we have fulfilled our purpose—or at least have had the opportunity to do so—we are claimed by death. Nothing or no one can circumvent that reality, not the least and the weakest among us nor the strongest and the greatest. And it is that reality that makes us all equal to one another, but not the same.

Being equal in one sense does not mean that we are the same in other ways. The obvious fact was that a tree was different than a blade of grass, a deer different than a snake or a bison, and so on. Obvious differences were in the categories of size, speed, and strength, but there were also the matters of lifestyle. Some animals were nocturnal, hunting and feeding at night, and some such as bison, caribou, birds, butterflies, and whales migrated. Others hibernated during the winter, like bears, toads, and frogs. Some functioned in more socially oriented groups or herds, such as wolves and bison, and some were loners, such as mountain lions.

Differences, however, were not regarded in terms of inferiority or superiority, because it was obvious to humans that every kind of being had at least one characteristic that set it apart, some more obvious than others. Skunks, as a case in point, had the unique defense of a noxious spray that made predators think twice. The same was true of porcupines with their sharp quills, which protruded like hairs along their back and tail, that could inflict painful wounds when impaled in anyone foolish enough to get too close. But there were other reasons than defense for some of the unique characteristics evolved by animals. Deer changed the color of their hair from summer tan to autumn gray, thus blending in more easily with autumn and winter landscapes. Arctic foxes turned snow white in the winter to camouflage themselves against the snowy landscape, thus improving their chances as hunters to catch their prey.

And where, in the estimation of humans, did humans fit in this scale of variety and diversity? Modern gun-toting, technology-backed humans who believe we have dominion over the earth might think we are at the top of the heap and have no need to "fit in" anywhere. But when the guns, four-wheel-drives, spotting scopes, and the sense of having dominion is taken away, humans rank pitifully low on the earth's-creature scale based on strength and speed. We have no claws; the only animal we can outrun for certain is the turtle; we have no fangs, and a so-so sense of smell and eyesight; and, left to our own devices, we would probably come away the loser in a one-on-one encounter with just about any creature bigger than a bread box. If our ancient ancestors had overlooked this reality, none of us would be here today. Fortunately for us, they were smart enough to accept how things were. That was an important step toward human survival and societal development.

Somewhere along the line, at some point in human societal evolution, people decided not to ignore the reality of their place in the natural environment. I doubt it was discussed at a grand council with edicts announced as the law of the clan. It was more than likely conceived in small realizations brought on by lessons learned, probably the hard way most of the time. A female bear with cubs must be avoided, for example—a harsh reality more than likely stamped on the human psyche after a man or woman was killed by a protective sow. Fruits and berries are less offensive to the gastrointestinal tract when consumed ripe. Such lessons were learned all over the world and passed down to the next generation. Over time there was a continuum of knowledge that helped people tip the odds in favor of their survival. The power and wisdom of that knowledge was proven each time it worked, and, too, whenever someone decided to defy its logic.

I foolishly tried defiance when I was a boy. It was 1951, in the middle of a deep winter snow, and my grandfather and I were going home after a day of hunting. It was very cold and I was anxious to be where I knew it was warm and where a bowl of hot soup was waiting. So I suggested to my grandfather that we should cross a snow-filled gully, and cut the distance home by two-thirds.

My grandfather replied that it would not be safe to walk on the snow that filled the gully, even though we had watched a large jackrabbit lope across it. He pointed out that the top layer of crusted snow was not strong enough to bear my weight. That bit of information went in one ear and out the other and I followed the rabbit's tracks across the snow.

At the end of the snow bank, it curved in a pronounced ridge to the floor of the gully, a consequence of the wind. All of a sudden, I was swimming in soft snow after breaking through the crust. My grandfather let me ponder my situation for a moment or two before he rescued me from my own foolishness, and the frigid snow. Even now, having learned a simple lesson the hard way, I still give appropriate berth to snow-filled gullies and creeks, and I have never questioned my grandfather's knowledge and wisdom. But I also learned that it is a human frailty to question reality and learn respect the hard way. Sometimes it serves us, but it also reveals that we are not the most intelligent creatures on the face of the earth.

I doubt that the lesson I learned that winter day in the gully (and others throughout my upbringing as well) were any different than any learned by our ancient ancestors, if only because it taught me respect for the natural environment.

There is a hidden lesson as well. The consequence of respect is awareness of that which one has learned to respect. Until that day in my boyhood, I heard from both of my grandparents that snow behaved in different ways. My grandmother told of stepping down through encrusted snow and painfully gashing her shin. My grandfather cautioned not to trust river ice that had been covered by snow, because the ice beneath it was often not as thick and strong. Those insights and stories became meaningful after that day, and snow became more than something to ride a sled on. Snow was nothing to be messed with.

The same was true for other things in the natural world, and the sooner one learned that, the healthier one would remain. It was not until later that I heard my father make a comment about something that was an "old Indian trick." He was referring to knowing or doing something seemingly innocuous that made a radical difference. He had placed a sheet of cardboard in front of his car's radiator on a –20°F winter day. That simple trick enabled the water in the radiator to heat up faster and stay warm. Knowing and doing those kinds of things would enable me to live to be an old Indian, he told me.

He later taught me a more organic trick. Since my grandparents and I traveled by horse and wagon all year long, my father showed me where to look for old birds' nests so that I could collect several of them. Old birds' nests made the best kindling, according to him. If my grandparents and I ever needed to stop on a winter day and build a fire, the old nests would save us from having to scrounge for kindling, and we would have a fire going in no time. He was right. But what he neglected to tell me was that my grandfather already knew it.

What is the point to these stories? Other than pointing out that we are not that much different than our ancestors—no matter how far we look back—it is important to understand that humans developed their knowledge base about the natural environment over time. It did not all come down in one or two generations. One little trick led to another, as it were, improving one generation's odds of survival by just that much. As a practitioner of primitive archery and someone who is intensely interested in how our ancestors lived and survived day to day, one of the questions I frequently ponder is how the bow and arrow came to be. That question is best answered when we understand that things came about and were improved either by necessity or by accident. But, to me, how the bow and arrow might have come into existence is indicative of how ancient man came to respect the earth and developed a spiritual bond with it.

Much of what we have and use today in terms of tools, weapons, and utensils have their origins in the ancient past, probably farther back in time than we realize. Firearms are descendants of bows and arrows because they are the continuation of the progression—improvement and refinement—of the concept of objects (projectiles) propelled by a power source. That being said, then throwing stones was the original idea, or perhaps even spitting. Someone probably had a "what if" moment that led to the implementation of an idea.

Throwing stones likely led to other means of sending objects. Throwing stones with slings was a definite improvement. The biblical story of David and Goliath is the easiest way to illustrate the power and effectiveness of the sling. Eventually spears with sharpened points became more effective at killing game and fighting enemies, and when flintknapping came along, sharpened stone points were attached to the point of the spear. Then came the atlatl, which is simply a long-handle that casts a spear (also called a dart though it is up to six feet in length) that enabled the thrower to propel it greater distances, perhaps up to ten times farther than with his arm alone. The atlatl dart or spear was the forerunner of the arrow. The dart is a slender shaft, tipped at one end with a sharpened stone point, with feathers attached at the other to enable stable flight. Arrows are smaller versions.

The same kinds of tools and weapons and processes were invented in different human societies all over the world, as indicated by the widespread use of stone knives and projectile points, though obviously not simultaneously. In societies living in jungles with access to bamboo, a large hollow grass, the blow gun was invented: a small, very slender dart inserted into one end of a long, hollow tube, propelled by blowing. Therefore, the use and refinement of projectiles of various types was worldwide.

Someone or some group somehow came up with the bow—the ends of a bent stick connected by a cord or a string—to use as the basic tool for drilling holes and starting fires. The basic components of it were the bent stick and string, a slender shaft tipped with a sharp stone, roughly in the shape of what we now know as an arrowhead, as the drill bit, and a guide plate made of wood that fit into a man's palm to hold the bit in place. A guide hole was carved into the guide plate.

The bow drill was operated by twisting the drill shaft into the string, then the bow was pulled back and forth in line with the string, which in turn rotated the drill shaft back and forth. Pushing the bow rotated the drill shaft several times and pulling it back rotated it in the opposite direction, and was continued until the hole was drilled. This was a simple tool with basic components, though it took (and takes) a certain amount of practice to operate it smoothly and effectively.

A simple change of the shaft to one that was slightly thicker and with only a sharpened point and it became a fire starter. A piece of base wood was added, of either hardwood or soft wood. The shaft was rotated, as before, until the friction between it and the base created tiny hot embers that fell onto light kindling below, usually dry grass. The operator blew gently on the tiny embers, coaxing them into flame.

The bow that made both the drill and the fire starter possible was used for hundreds and even thousands of years, just as the atlatl had been used as a dart and spear thrower, waiting to evolve into a new kind of weapon. We will never know when that happened, but it likely occurred because someone accidentally realized that the bow with its string could propel the shaft. Perhaps this was followed by another "what if" moment.

At some point in time someone had to have placed the dart (the atlatl spear) against the string of the bow, and pulled back and released just to see what would happen. Perhaps it was done again and again until the idea eventually took hold that a smaller dart would be better. And so it was.

In any case, that is my theory and I am sticking to it.

What we do know is that the dart became thinner and shorter and evolved into an arrow, and the bow became larger, and together these two items created the weapon of choice for hunters and warriors all over the world for thousands of years.

A good idea, a philosophy, a belief, and the acceptance of reality evolve in much the same way. Given that they were in direct contact with the natural environment practically every waking moment of their lives, indigenous ancestors knew or believed that everything else was based on it or was connected to it. As their values and societal norms developed, so did their respect for their world—the natural environment they were part of.

Therein was the foundation for their relationship with Grandmother Earth. They realized they were part of it and not in control of it. They also realized the realities of the natural environment did not negotiate or alter themselves to suit human needs. This is something we have apparently forgotten. But perhaps the most profound reality was that the human ability to reason was no more powerful than the characteristics that gave other forms of life a chance at survival.

In other words, our fang or claw, our strength or speed, our basic chance at survival was our ability to reason.

Through reasoning, we could also emulate

animals. He could imitate them to increase his success at hunting, and therefore his chances at survival. My favorite example is this story of how men learned to hunt like wolves.

Men could not improve their sense of smell, or their hearing and eyesight, or achieve the physical endurance the wolf possessed. Wolves could pursue prey for days, often with very little rest. To be more like the wolf, humans could use their own native endurance and improve upon it, and be in touch with their immediate surroundings. But the one wolf characteristic that many tribes in pre-European North America used was the ability to persevere. Wolves obviously lived by hunting, as did our indigenous ancestors. Though wolves failed more often than they succeeded, they never gave up. That was well within the man's ability to learn and use.

There were any number of ways by which the natural environment could thwart, defeat, and even kill humans. The most effective way to negate the power of Mother Nature was to learn and accumulate knowledge, to know how the natural environment functioned and behaved in any season and any circumstance, to know the cause and effect parameters by which it functioned. Consequently, in learning how to survive within those parameters, man came to respect the natural environment. He slowly began to realize that life on earth was not something to be constantly faced, contested, or fought against. Inevitably at some point he thought of the world on which he lived and moved as Grandmother Earth, and felt connected to her.

That sense of connection was the common thread that wove itself through many different indigenous North American cultures. It was, and is, more than a philosophy. A philosophy is thought, and believed. But in the case of ancient indigenous people, man's connection to his natural environment is real, is lived, and remains relevant.

AFTERWORD: WHEN WE RETURN TO YOU

There is a grave on a west-facing hillside above the Little White River, two miles west of where our log house once stood. The log house is long gone and the exact location of the grave is unknown, but both are firmly fixed in my memory. Both are indicators that we serve the earth best, and most respectfully, when we leave little or nothing behind that mars the natural environment.

My grandmother told me about the grave when I was still a boy. It is her father's final resting place, but there is no marker to identify or locate it. It is, she said, the way her father wanted it. He was a traditional healer, a medicine man named Good Voice Eagle, and my great grandfather.

According to her, he was buried without a casket, wrapped only in blankets and robes. He wanted nothing to impede his return to the soil, because his journey would not be over until he was one with the earth. Then, and only then, would the cycle of his life be completed. And thus it was.

"It is your embrace we feel," the prayer says, "when we return to you."

My great-grandfather understood that simple phrase. But it is more than a phrase, or a primitive belief, or a philosophy, or hope. It is profound reality, the basis for how pre-European cultures in North America look at the human relationship with the earth. So many of us do not understand that to ignore that reality is not to circumvent it. Furthermore, many of us—if not most of us—do not realize that ignoring reality has brought us to a moment of profound uncertainty in our existence as a species.

Somewhere in the time line of human societal evolution, our attitude toward nature changed from coexistence to control. Perhaps that moment occurred when people realized that planting seeds and raising crops was more dependable than gathering wild fruits and vegetables, where availability and quantity depended on uncontrollable factors. Planting crops was a significant alteration, a way to control the odds of survival. Control became the larger lesson, one that likely became the basis of human interaction with the natural environment thereafter. If one aspect of survival, of interaction with nature, could be changed and controlled, they had to have thought that it was possible in other ways as well. They probably sooner or later realized that, as farmers, they were forced to rely on unpredictable weather to bring rains to enable crops to grow. The concept of bringing water to the crops without depending on rain was every bit a major milestone as planting. After countless generations of hauling water from streams and rivers, the idea of actually altering the flow of a stream to sustain crops led to the beginnings of irrigation. On the surface, such evolutionary leaps enabled humans to survive and thrive, but it also affirmed and reaffirmed the illusion that they could control the natural environment.

As humans achieved more and increased their ability to alter the ways in which they could affect the natural environment for their own comfort, the idea of dominion over nature became further ingrained. Eventually that sense translated into more and more evidence of the human footprint on the face of the earth. Trails became wider roads after they were cleared of obstacles and then laid out to shorten the distance between two points. A simple log bridge over a stream became a wider structure to support greater loads, and then men saw the possibility of spanning wider and wider streams. With every achievement, dominion over the natural environment became a tangible fact and part of the human psyche. Coexistence with it was no longer a necessary approach.

When human groups thrive, human population grows, and so does its impact on the natural environment. Bigger and more permanent dwellings required more trees to be cut down. Bigger villages meant that domesticated animals, such as cattle and pigs, also had an impact on the land. Thus the swath of consumption and alteration of the natural environment grew in direct relation to the growth of human population. Today there are few places on the surface of the planet that do not bear the mark or evidence of human habitation or impact. Pristine wilderness is the exception rather than the rule.

And sadly, we have also polluted the atmosphere around the planet and the space beyond it. While we watch television and talk on cellular phones whose signals are conveyed by satellites, we tend not to think of the space junk orbiting our planet along with communication satellites. Our impact knows no limits, which coincides with our sense of control over our environment—be it beneath our feet or over our heads. Now much of that impact is actively destructive. As global warming and other looming environmental problems become more of a reality every day, we are pointing fingers. We need someone to blame.

Many of us think that since "they" are the chief

cause of global warming, for instance, "they" should come up with the solutions. The trouble is, no one has yet ascertained exactly who "they" are. What most of us do not yet understand is that it is not only corporations and big businesses or the indifference of governments that contribute to the impact we humans continue to have on our planet. The truth is that we all contribute to it each and every day because of our attitudes and our lifestyles.

Nearly thirty years ago I listened to a geophysicist assuring his dinner partner that man could not possibly do enough harm to the earth to cause profound changes in the natural environment. He was responding to a comment about a scientific article in a major magazine about the hole in the ozone layer caused by carbon dioxide emissions, and the possible consequences for life on the planet. In his opinion, the earth was too tough and the article was nothing more than conjecture. I wonder what that scientist's reaction is to the current body of apparent evidence that indicates global warming is happening.

Most of us are not scientists, but I fear that most of us do think that we are not so much to blame for the negative impacts on the environment as others. We continue to ignore what we, individually, are doing to it.

Each person in the United States creates 150 pounds of trash every month, which translates into billion of tons nationwide. Most of this finds its way to open dumps. We are a "use and dispose" culture, blithely unaware that the plastic water bottle we throw into the trash bin today will not decay for about seven hundred years. Too many of us don't have the slightest inclination to dispose of that bottle into a recycling bin, where its possible adverse impact on the environment is decreased. Too many of us are not aware, or do not care, that recycling any material reduces the demand we constantly place on our planet's limited natural resources. The truth is, we do not respect the planet.

Much of what we learn as individuals and societies is passed down to us from the previous generation. The previous generation, of course, learned it from the one before. Thus how we think and behave is influenced by the past, whether or not we in the present are aware of that reality. Consequently, when we are taught about great engineering feats—such as the building of the Panama Canal, the Golden Gate Bridge, the Big Dig, the Chunnel, and the Dutch sea locks and other such awe-inspiring accomplishments—what we are really learning is the control man has achieved—or thinks he has achieved—over nature. And the more control we know or even simply think we have over something, the less we respect it.

Therefore, especially in the industrialized societies of the world, dominion over nature is an operative concept taught to many, many generations. "Man is powerful," is the message and perceived reality, "and even more powerful than nature." And respect is not part of that thinking.

If respect for the natural environment is not taught to us, we cannot apply it in our lives. At some point, we as individuals must learn to respect nature, because that is the first step in the answer to the environmental problems we face today. If we, as individuals, do not take the lead to correct the ages-old premise of dominion over nature, and demonstrate that there is much to be gained from a realistic and respectful interaction with our environment, our governments will continue to be indifferent to many of the most threatening aspects of environmental degradation, and, worse, they will be at the mercy of the interests who have much to gain from man taking what he needs from the planet. Thankfully, the movement toward mindfulness is already in place. And the simple and effective acts of many individuals can become a powerful, positive impact on a large scale.

To counteract the alarming wrongs we have inflicted upon the earth, we need to understand how our ancient ancestors regarded the idea of coexisting with the earth. However, the first thing we need to do is not to arbitrarily assume that coexistence with the earth requires wholesale change. Coexistence is not anti-capitalistic, anti-American, or anti-comfort. It does not mean going back to dwelling in caves or cooking our meals over a campfire. Nor does it mean that automobiles and air-conditioning will cease to exist. It does mean, however, that how we provide those necessities and comforts will be done differently. If it means the end of the internal combustion engine, it does not mean the end of vehicular transportation. If it means a different kind of insulation for our homes, it does not mean that we cannot be warm. If it means using less toxic paint in and on our houses to eliminate health risks, it does not mean our homes will be less colorful or be less protected from the elements. But what coexistence with the earth does mean is a change in our thinking and our ways. We need to consider and follow my great-grandfather's example. We need to accept the reality of what we as a species have ignored for too many thousands of years: We are part of the earth, not apart from it.

As many times as I have visited the hillside where my grandmother said her father's grave is, I have never been able to locate it. Interestingly, however, there have been a few summers when a particular area has sprouted thicker and greener grass. As far as I am concerned, my great-grandfather's earthly remains are beneath that lush grass. I have never doubted that he was there, or at least his remains. But as a child I wondered why he did not want a casket, since as far as I knew that was how people were buried after they died. It seemed strange to me that he wanted something different. Only after I learned the reality of how my ancestors tried to exist within the parameters of the natural environment did I finally begin to understand. Whatever is beneficial to the natural environment is beneficial to humans. Conversely, anything bad for the earth is bad for humans. These are simple realities to live or die by.

Returning to the earth does not mean that we will become a part of the planet only when we die and our remains decompose back to the basic elements that formed us. Returning to the earth means adopting a mind-set while we are still alive that enables us to interact with the natural environment out of respect. A mind-set of arrogance may have enabled humans to make our lives and existence comfortable, but it has been at the expense of the earth. The ultimate demonstration of respect would be to use the ability, intelligence, technology, and persistence that split the atom, developed electronic communication, or created the great infrastructures that we regard as the crowning achievements of our respective cultures to find ways to exist and flourish within the realities that we have ignored.

Only then can we truly return to the earth.

ACKNOWLEDGMENTS

As I have often said to audiences I have spoken to, I profoundly wish I had paid much more attention to everything that both sets of my grandparents said to me, not to mention all the other elders that were part of my childhood and upbringing. If I had, there would be a good chance I might be wise someday. Nonetheless, it is they who are the reasons and sources for my outlook on life and the past, and for who and what I am as a person and a Lakota.

Though I spent the formative years of childhood with my maternal grandparents, Albert and Annie (Good Voice Eagle) Two Hawk, my paternal grandparents, the Rev. Charles and M. Blanche (Roubideaux) Marshall, had a significant and enduring impact on me as well. All of their places in my heart are more permanent than their photographs on my bookshelf.

The concept for this work had its beginning in 2005, primarily with Ms. Patty Gift, who was then a senior editor at Sterling. A heartfelt thank you to her, and no less to Michael Fragnito, who picked up the ball and put his considerable support behind it. A special thank you to Kate Zimmermann, my editor, who had to wade through the manuscript to figure out what I was trying to say. Also to everyone at Sterling who had a hand in the production and presentation of this book.

And of course, a very special thank you to my agent and chief motivator, my wife, Connie West, who makes the experience and the journey worthwhile. Last, but not least, thanks to my youngest daughter, Caitlin, who pitched in with a bit of research.

I hope that this book measures up to all of your efforts and support.

INDEX

Note: Page numbers in *italics* include illustrations.